ESTATE PLANNING MADE EASY

By Herbert F. Starr

D1073523

© Herbert F. Starr, 1984
LIBERTY PUBLISHING COMPANY
Cockeysville, Maryland

First Printing: December, 1984
Second Printing: October, 1985

Published by:

Liberty Publishing Company, Inc.
50 Scott Adam Road
Cockeysville, Maryland 21030

Library of Congress #83-82658
ISBN 0-89709-127-2

This publication is designed to provide accurate and authorative information in regard to the subject matter covered. It is sold with the understanding that the publisher is not engaged in rendering legal, accounting or other professional service. If legal advice or other expert assistance is required, the services of a competent professional person should be sought.—*From a Declaration of Principles jointly adopted by a Committee of the American Bar Association and a Committee of Publishers and Associations.*

Manufactured USA

To my wife Nancy

Table of Contents

Introduction 1
The Basic Art of Planning.................... 5
Establishing Your Goals...................... 9
Targeting a Goal; Legal/Administrative
Costs.. 15
Identifying Potential Legal/Administrative
Costs.. 19
Setting Up Your Plan 23
Eliminating Probate Costs.................... 25
Documenting an Estate's Assets 31
Preparing for Settlement Costs 35
The Revocable Living Trust 39
The Buy-Sell Agreement 43
Life Insurance............................... 47
A Summary of Legal/Administrative
Costs.. 51
Understanding Estate and Inheritance
Taxes.. 55
Reducing First Generation Taxes 63
Reducing Second Generation Taxes 71
The Estate Planner's Eight Basic Tools 77
The Marital Deduction....................... 81
Trusts in General 87
The Marital Trust 91
Pre-Death Gifts 95
Asset Sales 99
The Private Annuity......................... 101
Incorporation and Partnerships 103
How to Pay Taxes 107

Cash from the Estate 111
Post-Death Financing 113
Pre-Death Financing 117
Selecting the Right Option 121
Let the IRS Contribute to Its Own Estate
Tax Bill..................................... 125
A Summation 129
The United States Estate Tax................. 133
Appendix 141
Index 152

Introduction

Estate planning as a specific financial discipline has many definitions. But the concept can be simply stated:

> ESTATE PLANNING IS AN ORGANIZED
> EFFORT TO ATTAIN THE MAXIMUM
> ESTATE RETENTION FOR ONE'S HEIRS
> CONSISTENT WITH MAINTAINING ONE'S
> OWN FINANCIAL INDEPENDENCE
> AND SECURITY.

Probably the most common misconception about estate planning is the belief that it is an optional exercise. It is not! Federal and state laws demand an accounting of a decedent's estate and the payment of any attendant taxes. What IS optional is when and by whom the planning is done.

You, your wife (husband) and/or other heirs may plan NOW in a calm atmosphere while many dollar-saving options are open;

OR

You or your surviving spouse *must* carry out this responsibility immediately after a death, during a period of sadness and vulnerability when precious few dollar-saving options remain.

Another common misconception is that estate planning is a complex and time-consuming endeavor. Properly done, it is not!

Every effort has been made to keep this book as nontechnical as possible while providing you with the basics of planning and a general understanding of the tools of an estate planner.

I do not suggest that you use this information as a do-it-yourself guide nor are my comments and observations to be construed as specific legal advice.

I do believe, however, that when you finish this book you will be more than able to recognize whether your own technicians— be they accountants or attorneys—are truly professional estate planners!

More importantly, you will be fully capable of coordinating your own estate plan. You will come to realize that defining exactly what you wish to accomplish is not an abstruse legal matter and can be spelled out clearly in layman language.

Goal-oriented planning is the essence of sound business practice and management consulting. Goal-oriented planning also should be the essence of any effort at estate conservation.

Now, as never before, the techniques of the management consultant are essential to successful estate planning. The 1981 Economic Recovery Tax Act significantly reduced the number of estates subject to Federal estate taxes. Those affected are liable to become complacent and figure there no longer is a need for any planning beyond a basic last will and testament.

NOTHING COULD BE FURTHER FROM THE TRUTH!

First off, Federal taxes are but one part of estate conservation planning. The potential drain of excessive legal and administrative costs must be addressed. And there are other potential pitfalls, notably those related to implementing the terms of the will.

As you will see, the consultant's approach to estate planning—the basis of this text—is to ferret out *all* potential costs for systematic justification or elimination.

Management consulting concerns itself with the total picture. In assuming this role, you will determine what should be done and why it should be done. You will select the appropriate technician—accountant or attorney—and assign the necessary tasks.

This book is designed to prepare you fully for this consultant role in your own estate planning. A careful reading will enable you to clearly understand what must be done and why it must be done to "maximize estate retention for your heirs consistent with maintaining one's own financial independence and security."

You also will gain sufficient technical knowledge to monitor the specific tasks you assign your technicians. YOU will control the planning effort.

To attain that mastery requires only a modest sacrifice of your valuable time and a reasonable degree of concentration. This book is not something to be lightly skimmed or handed to a subordinate for a quick briefing. It is addressed to YOU— the man or woman of property—and deserves your personal attention.

The author welcomes your comments or questions.

HERBERT F. STARR

The Basic Art of Planning

If you were to check your dictionary you would find the word "plan" defined somewhat along this line: "A methodical arrangement of certain steps necessary to get you from where you are now to where you are going." It simply isn't possible to call any series of actions a plan unless they conform generally to this definition.

There is only one right way to plan for anything. Whether you are planning a birthday party, an estate transfer, a corporate merger or World War III—the same basic rules apply. They are as follows:

Rule I   *Establish Your Goal*—What is your objective? Where are you going?

Rule II   *Establish Your Present Position*—Where are you now in relation to that goal?

Rule III   *Establish A Specific Plan*—By identifying and arranging for the implementation of the specific steps necessary to bring you from your present position to your goal.

The rules applied to estate planning:

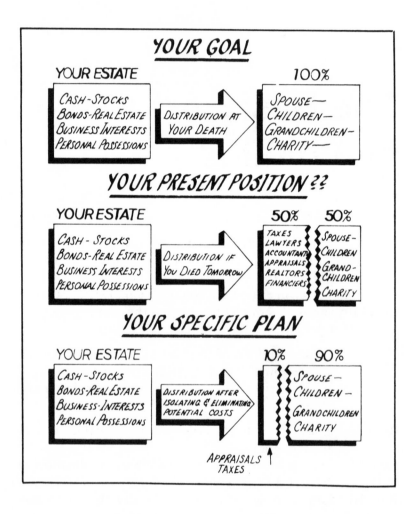

There is no other way to put together an intelligent plan. If you don't know where you are going (Rule I) and where you are now (Rule II), how can you possibly lay out a methodical series of steps to get you from where you are now to where you want to be (Rule III)?

TODAY'S TYPICAL PLANNER

For some reason these basic concepts, universally accepted in all other areas of business and financial planning, are unceremoniously abandoned in the typical estate planning effort.

The principal reason for this probably lies in the basic orientation of the typical estate planner, the attorney or CPA. Neither the attorney nor the accountant has by formal education or practical experience the specific skills that are required of a business (or estate) planner. An estate plan is, of course, simply one kind of business plan . . . a plan for the inevitable change of asset ownership.

The lawyer is a detail oriented legal technician. The accountant is a numbers oriented tax technician. Probably the most compelling evidence against the planning talents of our attorneys and accountants is their almost universal inability to get their own work done in a timely fashion.

TODAY'S PROFESSIONAL PLANNER

A planner must be a goal-directed, methodical organizer first and foremost. If he is also a technician, fine, if not he can hire one. The planner recognizes the primacy of establishing goals. He further recognizes that specific planning techniques should only be discussed within the framework of attaining those goals.

Finally, he recognizes that involving the layman in the legalistics of the planning techniques or tools is both unnecessary and counterproductive. The patient need not master the surgeon's craft to realize the benefits of the procedure.

While estate planning is indeed *not* a complex and time consuming effort under the auspices of a professional planner, it usually becomes so when under the control of the typical attorney or accountant.

Being unskilled in the ways of planning, they generally become mired in detail with the parts of an estate plan and fail to understand and/or communicate how each part fits into a total plan. Thus the client, deprived of an understanding of the big picture and immersed in details he couldn't care less about, soon becomes confused and discouraged.

At this point he will either abandon the whole project or, for better or worse, turn it over carte blanche to his attorney or accountant.

Another reason for complex and confusing planning might be attributed to the planner's lack of motivation for "maximizing your estate retention." You and your estate stand to benefit most from a sound estate plan.

The attorneys and accountants profit far more straightening out a mess later than they do preventing one now. Your estate's financial interests are diametrically opposed to the personal financial interests of your advisors. The very people you lean on for advice stand to lose to a large extent the very same dollars you stand to save.

To be sure, many attorneys and accountants keep your interest first; unfortunately, far too many do not. Most poor planning, however, is due more to nonfeasance than to malfeasance.

Let's now look at how the basic concepts of planning apply specifically to the financial discipline called "estate planning."

Establishing Your Goals

The general goal of every estate plan is "to maximize estate retention for one's heirs in a manner consistent with maintaining your own financial independence and security."

The specific goals you should set to accomplish this general goal will be based on an understanding of the following salient points.

Maximizing estate retention is accomplished by minimizing estate settlement costs. Such costs consist of any and all expenses incurred in transferring decedent's estate to his or her heirs. By far the largest portion of these costs fall into two major categories:

A) Federal and/or state taxes.
B) Legal and administrative expenses.

The typical estate, even with a well-drawn current will, experiences a shrinkage of anywhere from 25 to 50 percent or more due to transfer taxes and legal/administrative costs. Indeed most "allegedly" well planned estates suffer a loss of 5 to

10 percent or more due to legal and administrative costs alone. The *truly* well-planned estate incurs minimal taxation and virtually *no* legal and administrative costs.

BASIC GOALS

While the general goal of the estate planner is to maximize estate retention without jeopardizing your financial security or independence, there are three specific goals to establish in order to attain that end.

The *first goal* is simple, basic and mandatory for all estates. Everybody's first goal is the elimination of all nonessential legal and administrative expenses. Among such costs:

NON-ESSENTIAL COSTS

PROBATE FEES, EXECUTOR
PROBATE FEES, ATTORNEY
COURT FEES
BUSINESS INTEREST DISPOSITION
AUCTION FEES
REAL ESTATE LIQUIDATION COSTS
ANCILLARY ADMINISTRATION
FINANCING CHARGES
ASSET ACCUMULATION COSTS
BUSINESS INTEREST EVALUATIONS
WILL CONTESTS

ESSENTIAL COSTS

APPRAISALS
TAX FILING COSTS

The other two specific goals address saving taxes.

The *second goal* (discretionary) is a specific, pre-death reduction in the size of your estate in order to realize a reduction in "first generation" taxes; i.e., the initial estate taxation on your assets.

The *third goal* (discretionary) is a possible revision of your present distribution plans (your will) to minimize "second generation" taxes; i.e., the retaxation of your original estate in the estates of your spouse and children.

Estate planning for tax savings is concerned with both what *you* have when you die and what your heirs have of *yours* when they die.

In general, any taxes saved will be saved as a result of people being worth less at death than they would otherwise have been. Part of what would have been in their taxable estate is already in the possession of their heirs.

The name of the tax saving game is to transfer as much of your estate as you can before death and to direct as much estate, both before and after death, as far down your progeny as is practical in light of nontax considerations.

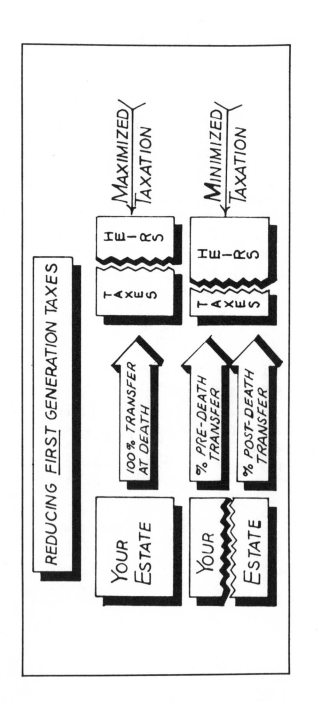

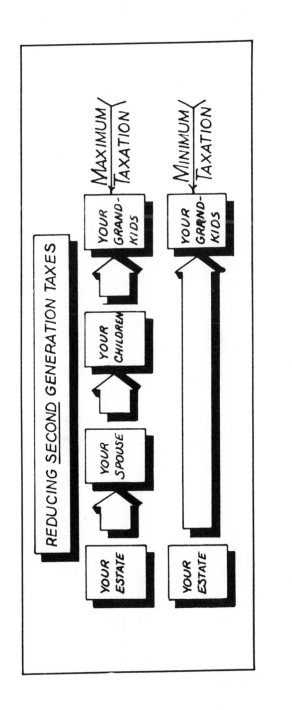

REDUCING SECOND GENERATION TAXES

YOUR ESTATE → YOUR SPOUSE → YOUR CHILDREN → YOUR GRAND-KIDS — MAXIMUM TAXATION

YOUR ESTATE → YOUR GRAND-KIDS — MINIMUM TAXATION

Targeting a Goal: Legal/Administrative Costs

Everybody's first estate planning goal is easy to identify but a bit more difficult to define. The choice of definitions lies between "the reduction of legal and administrative costs" and "the reduction of legal and administrative red tape." Legal costs and red tape, of course, go hand in hand. Most estates, particularly the smaller ones, incur far more problems with administration than taxes. As a rule, people planning their estate transfer think taxes, taxes, taxes. Heirs, however, tend to remember all the red tape and legal costs.

THE COMPLEXITIES

Bewildered heirs are generally about evenly divided between those frustrated by the seemingly endless legal procedures and those simply shocked by the extent of nontax legal and administrative expenses involved.

On one side some people suggest they gladly would have paid even more if it would have simplified the procedure and expedited the ultimate transfer of the estate's assets. Month after month after month of constant interruption in their day-to-day life to sign this, answer that, research this, discuss that had indeed taken its toll. To these people the cost in dollars was not entirely unexpected, but the cost in terms of personal wear and tear was a most unwelcome annoyance.

THE COSTS

On the other side are those who possibly had more time than money. While they expected the taxes, they were not prepared for the seemingly endless stream of bills from attorneys, accountants, attorneys, appraisers, attorneys, etc.

Whatever the case, all are in accord with these comments from one exasperated heir: "Grandpa died, he left a will, what in the name of all that is good and holy was all that time and money spent on? If people die every day, why is it still so complex, confusing and costly simply to transfer their assets to their designated heirs?"

The fact that most estate transfers are complex, confusing and costly does *not* mean that they have to be. The ultimate in frustration sets in when one realizes that 90 percent of what they went through was totally avoidable with a little basic pre-death planning.

The target of every estate planner should be a smooth, efficient, relatively cost free transfer. This goal is indeed attainable, if you address the issue now.

THE LONG & COSTLY ROAD

Identifying Potential Legal/Administrative Costs

By definition, before you can organize a coordinated plan to attain your goals, you first must determine where you are now in relation to those goals. As to your goal of eliminating legal and administrative expenses, "Your Present Position" poses this specific question: If you or your wife died tomorrow, what would be the exact nature and approximate dollar amount of the costs attendant to settling the estate?

THE IDEAL ORGANIZATIONAL FORMAT

There is a standard form that the IRS will ultimately use to get these answers—The U.S. Estate Tax Return, Form 706. Tax determination depends in part on a complete accounting of all settlement costs.

Filing Form 706 will be the personal responsibility of your estate's executor if the assets are transferred by will or devolve upon your successor trustee if they are transferred by living trust. In either case, the completion of a Form 706 ultimately will provide the specific answers that we would like to have *now* . . . answers as to the exact nature and dollar amount of the legal and administrative costs attendant to settling the estate.

As long as Form 706 serves the purpose *after* death—why not use it now?

There is no better way to determine where you are now than by taking a "dry run" and completing a U.S. Estate Tax Return. The forms are available at any IRS office. Your attorney and accountant probably have them in stock too.

Since the federal estate tax is a simple net worth tax, you will find the 706 far less complex than the more familiar income tax form 1040.

If you are married you will want to complete a separate 706 for you and your spouse.

In every estate planning effort the first appointment scheduled with a technical "expert"—your attorney or accountant—should be for the sole purpose of completing these 706 forms!

Be sure to emphasize to your tax expert that the specific and limited purpose of this appointment is the completion of "mock" estate tax forms. The meeting is *not* being scheduled to seek solutions but solely to identify the nature and scope of the problem. Inquire as to what if any documents you should bring along.

Your number one priority at this meeting is the item by item identification of all likely legal and administrative expenses. They are to be specifically listed on Form 706 schedules J & L.

CONTROLLING THE PLANNING SESSION

Be sure you confine this meeting to addressing schedules J

and L until your advisor is satisfied he has identified all potential legal and administrative expenses.

This is quite possibly the single most important planning session you will have! Remember, these costs are the specific target of the first goal of everybody's estate plan . . . "the elimination of all nonessential legal and administrative expenses." These costs do in fact consume anywhere from 5 to 10 percent or more of the unplanned, or poorly planned estate. The procedures that generate those costs also prolong and complicate final settlement.

Once you and your advisor are content that schedules J and L are as accurate and complete as is practically possible, go on and complete the 706 to arrive at the federal taxes due. You will need this figure later when considering tax-saving goals.

Your next step in ascertaining "Your Present Position" is a radical step for an accountant or attorney to suggest, but a matter-of-course step for a business executive or management consultant to insist upon.

The wise and successful business planner never acts upon the input of one sole technician. Take your completed 706 and schedule one or two separate sessions with totally independent tax experts for the sole purpose of critiquing schedules J and L.

After these reviews you can confidently state that you have "Established Your Present Position"; i.e., identified exactly what it would cost to transfer your estate if you died tomorrow.

Incidentally, do not omit those reviews in deference to your attorney or accountant's feelings. None of us have all the answers. The advisor who puts your interests ahead of his ego should welcome this additional input.

Setting Up Your Plan

In keeping with the planning techniques of the management consultant, you have defined your goal—the reduction of legal and administrative expenses. You have identified your present position in relation to that goal—the legal and administrative expenses your death would generate today—through completion of our mock 706 return. It is now time to lay out the specific steps to get from where you are now to where you want to be . . . to establish a plan to eliminate all unnecessary legal and administrative expenses.

COMMON CAUSE, COMMON SOLUTION

Be assured that estate planning need not be a complex and time-consuming endeavor. As we begin now to define and resolve each of your three specific estate conservation goals this will become more and more apparent.

To begin with, your first goal is the same as everyone's—the reduction of legal and administrative expenses. Additionally, in virtually every estate better than 90 percent of these costs are attributable to the same three root causes. Upon review of schedule J on your dry run 706, you'll find that, in the main, these expenses consist of:

1) The cost of transferring assets through the Probate Court.
2) The cost of locating and evaluating an estate's assets.
3) The cost of acquiring necessary cash liquidity.

In all but the most complex of estates, these unnecessary costs are eliminated through the implementation of *the same three estate planning tools* . . . the living trust, the buy-sell agreement and life insurance.

Over the next three chapters we will examine each of the root causes in turn. In each case, we will show why the specific planning tool indicated will eliminate the particular legal or administrative cost.

Having done so, the succeeding three chapters will take a closer look at the workings of each of the three specific planning tools. The application of these three basic planning tools—the living trust, buy-sell agreements, life insurance—to your particular estate is your individualized plan for eliminating nonessential legal and administrative expenses.

Eliminating Probate Costs

The way to eliminate the costs of probate is to simply place your estate outside the jurisdiction of the Probate Court. This is best accomplished by putting your assets in a revocable (intervivos) living trust.

Rather than have the probate court transfer title to your assets after you die, *you* "transfer" title to the trust before you die. Your living "transfer" is revocable while you are alive but is an immediate irrevocable fact accomplished at your death.

However, before taking steps to avoid probate, it behooves you to know exactly what probate is—what it costs (schedule J of your IRS 706), and why its facilities may be of value to you.

Essentially, probate is a legal proceeding wherein the Probate Court becomes intimately involved in every facet of the transfer of a decedent's assets. The open court proceedings usually take from one to two or three years and can be very costly (again—see schedule J of your completed "dry run" Estate Tax Return).

From the filing of your will to an itemized listing and appraisal of your every asset; through a detailed accounting of your every creditor up to and including the actual specific distribution of your holdings—everything becomes a matter of permanent public record. Throughout the process the heirs can't even as much as sell off a few shares of stock without a specific court order. Once a probate file is opened, the estate's affairs are forever more in the public domain.

THE VALUE OF PROBATE??

The state bar of California, in various pamphlets, has suggested the purposes of probate are:

1. To determine your valid last will
2. Safeguard your spouse and minor children's rights
3. Protect your creditors' rights
4. Pay any estate or inheritance taxes due
5. To determine who gets your property
6. To oversee the work of your executor
7. Let your creditors know you have died
8. Supervise the sale of any property you said should be sold
9. See that debts and attorneys' fees are paid

In some states probate estate transfers may preclude future lawsuits where living trust estate transfers do not. Such cases are extremely rare. If probate is suggested on this basis, be sure to determine exactly who might sue your estate for exactly what. Actually, probate publicly solicits creditors and is subject to far more claims—nuisance and serious—than a living trust transfer, a considerably more private affair.

There are cases where income tax advantages may accrue through "dragging out" the probate process for two or three years. While the probate estate is a separate "income tax" taxpayer, the IRS is increasingly vigilant against such delaying tactics. If income tax savings through probate is suggested, be sure to have a detailed comparative cost analysis between the income taxes saved and the probate costs incurred. Let's emphasize the word DETAILED.

As a rule, immediate possession by the heirs affords far greater income tax planning opportunities. Total objectivity in your planning now would suggest you ASK YOUR HEIRS if they would prefer immediate possession or a drawn out probate.

Upon reviewing the bar's suggested advantages or benefits of probate, a client suggested: "We spend all our lives complaining about too much government in our lives. Throughout my life I have endeavored to minimize governmental involvement in my personal financial affairs. To suggest that I, having the option *not* to, should invite the Probate Court to conduct what amounts to a public inquisition over my final wishes is incongruous."

"To suggest, as the California Bar does, that I do it to protect the interests of the tax collectors, creditors and attorneys is the ultimate in absurdity. Were the entire probate process free, I would be willing to spend a fortune to avoid it."

The Probate Court may not be the "chamber of horrors" it is sometimes called. It is, nevertheless, in almost all cases a totally unnecessary and expensive ritual of legalistic mumbo-jumbo. Nobody requires you to go through probate. Neither the IRS, State taxing authorities or indeed the Probate Court itself have that authority. The decision is entirely yours and is contingent on the type of will you select:

> ## THE TRADITIONAL "LAST WILL AND TESTAMENT" IS SUBJECT TO PROBATE. THE "LIVING TRUST" WILL IS *NOT* SUBJECT TO PROBATE.

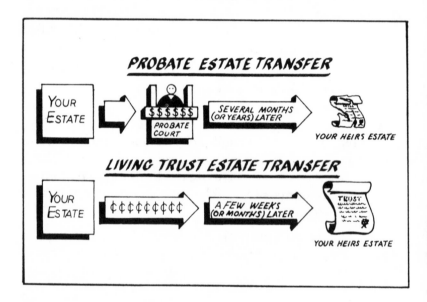

THE CHOICE IS YOURS

Should your advisors recommend probate over a living trust, insist on a written synopsis of the reasons why. Such a document should include, but not necessarily be limited to:

A list of specific disadvantages you or your heirs may anticipate as a result of your living trust.

A list of the specific advantages your heirs would enjoy as a result of using the probate court.

One final caution if your advisors are recommending probate. Frequently, when addressing the comparative merits of probate estate transfers vs. living trust estate transfers, the wrong positions are defended.

Probate court advocates emphasize what is "not wrong" with our reformed probate process when, in fact, they should be attempting to point out what is "right" about the process.

Nothing is right about the process in the sense that, almost without exception, nothing is accomplished in probate that cannot be accomplished via the living trust in a fraction of the time and for a fraction of the cost.

Using the same inverse logic, probate advocates will downplay the value of the living trust on the basis of what it does *not* do. The right question to ask in evaluating the living trust is: What does it do? Does it eliminate the delays and costs of probate without imposing any negatives on you now or your heirs after your death? The answer to that question is yes— again, in virtually every case.

Just about everything written on the subject acknowledges probate takes longer, costs more and, in general, is a far more tedious exercise for the heirs than the living trust transfer.

You will look far and wide to encounter anyone with fond memories of a Probate Court. You will even have to look farther to find one with negative experiences encountered because of a PROFESSIONALLY PREPARED living trust.

Documenting an Estate's Assets

Often the total scope of a decedent's estate is unknown to his heirs, the executor, and the executor's attorney. Most wills, after a few specific bequests, merely direct that the remainder estate after payment of just debts and taxes be allocated on a percentage basis to specific heirs.

What *is* the remainder? The estate executor and attorney are legally bound to search out and record the total estate. They can be held personally liable for taxes *not* paid due to incomplete reporting on the Federal and State death tax forms. Accumulating, documenting and evaluating a decedent's assets can be a time-consuming and costly exercise.

Such costs are strictly nonessential. They are completely eliminated during the establishment of your living trust. All your assets are accumulated and documented by the one who knows best—*you*—for inclusion in the inventory of assets section of the trust.

You do not have to include all your assets in the trust to effectively eliminate probate. For example, a joint tenancy checking account will bypass probate and also preclude any check cashing difficulties that may be caused by your rather cumbersome legal name, "John Doe, Trustee."

Aside from such a checking account there is no reason *not* to put everything in the trust; the simplicity of accumulating and documenting one's entire estate dictates total asset inclusion in the trust.

For the most part there is little a planner can do to reduce the ultimate costs incurred in evaluating an estate's assets. The IRS and state inheritance tax authorities pretty much dictate the nature and extent of any required appraisals.

One exception for the planners, and a significant one at that, involves the evaluation of a "closely held business" interest. Private business interests, be they of a corporate or partnership nature, have an inherent "intangible value" factor. This unique characteristic renders them rather difficult to evaluate in any case, let alone immediately after a death.

As a result, major legal and administrative costs commonly accompany both the evaluation and transfer of such assets.

A prearranged formula for evaluation and transfer of these business interests, the buy-sell agreement, offers a solution to this potentially serious problem. The buy-sell agreement is in its essence a business will or business continuation plan.

The implementation of buy-sell agreements, if applicable to your estate, is definitely a job for your CPA and attorney. While of necessity this is a rather complex document, a layman's explanation appears in a subsequent chapter.

THE LOOSE ENDS

A couple of final steps need to be taken to eliminate nonessential costs in accumulating, documenting and evaluating a decedent's assets.

Always maintain a written summary (updated annually) of all outstanding debts and mortgages. This can be invaluable for the heirs in honoring just claims against the estate.

Additionally, financial instruments of a named beneficiary nature such as certain annuities, pension and retirement plans, and life insurance policies, should be reviewed annually. A written inventory of these documents should be kept.

This written inventory should also include a summarized explanation of the various benefits the heirs could expect from each of the itemized documents.

Preparing for Settlement Costs

Federal taxes, State taxes, and just about any other estate settlement costs are cash demands against the estate.

One of the most common methods of providing the necessary cash is through asset liquidation. The subject of how to pay your settlement costs is addressed thoroughly in a later chapter. Here we will look at the asset liquidation method solely as it relates to legal and administrative expenses.

Converting a legitimate $100,000 nonliquid asset to cash is *not* a dollar for dollar exchange. Many planners fail to address this fact at all. The difference between the $100,000 asset and the actual net cash realized from its sale equals the cost of acquiring the cash.

Inasmuch as raising the cash is an administrative function, quite logically the cost is an administrative expense. It is a nontax cost that must be identified. It can and usually should be eliminated.

The procedure involved in converting nonliquid assets into cash is called an estate sale. Probably nothing excites a bargain hunter more than an estate sale. If ever big ticket items are to be bought at rock bottom prices, the estate sale is the place.

Obviously, the buyer's gain is the seller's loss. Actually, the seller's loss is even greater than the buyer's gain as the seller is responsible for the broker's or agent's fees and commissions.

FOR PURPOSES OF ILLUSTRATION:

Liquidity needs dictate that John Doe's widow (and co-trustee of their living trust) sell a rental house they own. Similar houses have sold recently for $100,000 while others have been on the market for some time.

With time not on her side (the estate taxes must be paid) she accepts an offer of $85,000 cash. Her listing broker extracts his $5,000 sales commission and Mrs. Doe receives $80,000 cash. Mrs. Doe has just incurred a $20,000 administrative expense.

In order to eliminate the administrative cost of acquiring necessary cash you must have either the cash itself on hand (frequently provided by life insurance) or assets that can readily be converted to cash *dollar for dollar.*

Be sure section J of your mock 706 identifies any potential legal and administrative costs attendant to raising cash for taxes, funeral expenses, etc.

The following illustration shows the *hidden* cost of raising cash through asset liquidation:

ASSET SOLD	CURRENT MARKET VALUE [1]	LIQUIDATION PRICE [2]	CASH LOST [3]	LEGAL FEES & COMMISSION [4]	NET CASH RECIEVED [5]
REAL PROPERTY	50000 —	40000 —	⟨10000⟩	⟨3000⟩	37000 —
ART WORKS	20000 —	15000 —	⟨5000⟩	⟨1500⟩	13500 —
BUSINESS INTEREST	60000 —	40000 —	⟨20000⟩	⟨2500⟩	37500 —
BONDS, ETC.	13000 —	12000 —	⟨1000⟩	-0-	12000 —
TOTALS			⟨36000⟩	⟨7000⟩	100000 —

$43,000

ADMINISTRATIVE COSTS INCURRED IN RAISING THE NEEDED CASH.

Once again, there are but three basic planning tools used to eliminate some 90 percent of an estate's potential legal and administrative expenses. The following pages provide an informed layman's explanation of the technical aspects of these tools—the revocable living trust, the business buy-sell agreement and life insurance.

The Revocable Living Trust

A revocable living trust is a legal entity which serves both as a title-holding company for your assets and your personal last will and testament. It is used primarily to avoid probate.

As a "holding company," the living trust becomes the technical owner of all your assets. John Doe no longer owns anything—all his assets are "gifted," revocably and without any gift taxes, to the trust.

When John Doe dies, the trust doesn't. Since his assets were transferred to the trust before he died and the probate process is only concerned with assets transferred *after* death, there is nothing to probate.

As a will, the living trust functions exactly the same as the traditional will. While you are alive you can revoke it or amend its terms; once you die, it becomes an irrevocable directive for the distribution of the assets.

The distribution of your assets, payment of taxes and other just claims is handled by the trust's "successor" trustee—a position akin to the executor in a probate court "will" transfer.

The estate's business is usually wound up in a matter of weeks as opposed to years in probate.

The costs are but a fraction of the costs of a probate court transfer, particularly if your state like California has a statutory fee schedule based on a percentage of the *GROSS* estate accounted for.

While mortgages and other debts do reduce your net worth (taxable estate), they *do not* reduce California's statutory probate fee base. Probate fees, based on the GROSS estate accounted for, are awarded by law to both the executor and the attorney, even when an attorney acting as executor hires his law partner as "legal counsel."

TRANSFER VEHICLES

Though the living trust serves as the primary asset distribution vehicle, a simply drawn will also is necessary. This so-called "pickup will" accompanies the living trust document in order to transfer any assets omitted from the trust or which might have accrued to the estate after death; e.g., proceeds from a wrongful death settlement.

So much for a living trust as a probate "substitute." Let's now look at "living" in a living trust.

Essentially, the revocable living trust is a three-part legal document simply titled, "The John Doe Trust."

PART ONE is "The Declaration of Trust." It names the grantor of the assets to the trust; names the current and successor trustees (managers); defines the rights, duties, limitations and obligations of said trustees; and establishes the current beneficiaries of the trust.

PART TWO is the specific inventory of assets that the grantor is putting in the trust. Deeds, stock certificates, bonds, bank accounts, etc., must be retitled into the trust's name.

PART THREE is the statement of the grantor's final wishes—his will—his distribution statement.

While you live, acting as your own trustee, you retain complete and total control over the trust with full rights to alter, amend, or revoke it. You enjoy complete access to its income. In short, you suffer no disadvantages as a result of the trust.

As long as you are competent to handle your own affairs, you should continue to act as your own trustee. In some states it is legally advisable to have a co-trustee, but you retain power of appointment over your co-trustee.

LIVING IN A LIVING TRUST

Basically, while acting as your own trustee, all you need to do is remember in your legal dealings you are known as "John Doe, Trustee" instead of "John Doe." The technician who sets up your trust will explain the few (but important!) new guidelines with which you will live.

From a practical day-to-day standpoint, there are no changes in the way you go about your business. Your financial decision-making process is unchanged but the "forms" of execution are implemented by you as "trustee" instead of simply under your signature.

It is highly advisable to give a professional trustee, such as a bank, a year or two of managing your trust *now*—IF you can foresee that you or your heirs will need professional financial management services in the future. Let a future trustee demonstrate his expertise to you while you are still around and alert enough to evaluate his work. For all the details and specifics, talk to a few bank trust officers in your area.

Your financial affairs are every bit as confidential in the living trust as they are now. Your banker, stockbroker, and real estate brokers, insurance companies, etc., may request copies of your trust.

What they need is PART I—the declaration of trust in order to satisfy legal technicalities in your "new" relationship. Under no circumstances, however, do they need access to the inventory of assets or the will section (PARTS II and III) of your living trust document.

TAX IMPLICATIONS

There are no Federal estate tax or gift tax ramifications in the establishment of a living trust. You haven't really parted with anything as far as the IRS is concerned. The State of California, in the wake of massive property tax reductions (Proposition 13) attempted to reassess real estate placed in revocable living trusts.

However, California AB 1488, effective July 10, 1979, ruled such transfers do not constitute a change of ownership (an act allowing reassessment). These facts alone demonstrate conclusively that, while you have "gifted" your assets to the living trust, they still belong to you and you alone.

Just about the only cost difference in setting up a standard will and a living will should be whatever additional time it takes your attorney to retitle your assets into the trust; in general, a few hours at the most. In drawing up either type of will, 90 percent of the wording is standard nomenclature and the total effort should run from 5 to 10 hours for all but the most complex estates.

Provisions should be made to insure that copies of your living trust "will" are made available to all your designated heirs upon your death. Your bank trust department might be willing to hold copies of your trust for such distribution.

The Buy-Sell Agreement

Through establishment of the revocable living trust you effectively eliminate both the cost of probate and the added cost of accumulating and documenting your assets. Should those assets include close corporation stock or business partnership interests, there could be a problem in *evaluating* said interests.

If an evaluation formula has not been established before death, you can be sure the decedent's heirs, the surviving stockholders, and the IRS are going to have three different ideas as to the value of the decedent's holdings. Arriving at a mutually acceptable figure is usually a lengthy and costly exercise.

This potentially serious problem is eliminated by the implementation of a business continuation plan, or "buy-sell agreement."

AN ABSOLUTE NECESSITY

Never, never, never enter into *any* business partnership or close corporation without a buy-sell agreement. You may get along

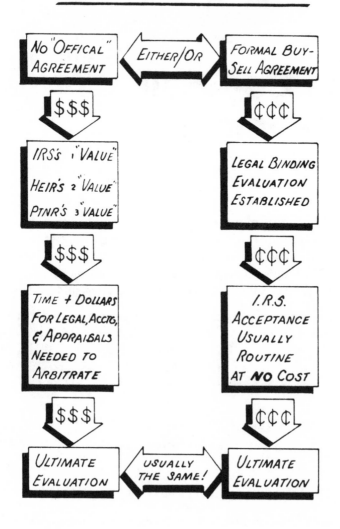

EVALUATING A DECEDENT'S BUSINESS INVESTMENT

fine with your associates, Richard and Susan Roe, but suppose they both die in an auto accident? You might then be dealing with their nephews and nieces. If there are several partners in a venture, the death of any one can cause untold grief for all of them.

The wisdom of an individual having a current distribution plan, through a will or living trust, is virtually self-evident. The fact that the death of any one business partner can cause problems for *all* the survivors suggests that a business will is at least equally important.

A buy-sell agreement need be nothing more than a few paragraphs in the partnership agreement or articles of incorporation.

Such agreements made "before the fact" establish fairly and objectively:

1. How a business interest is to be evaluated and transferred if one wants to sell out. A clause generally provides for a "first right of refusal" for the remaining owners.
2. How a business interest is to be evaluated upon a partner's death as well as if and how said interest is to be redeemed (optionally or by mandate) by the surviving owners or any other interested party. The interest may simply be transferred to the decedent's heirs.

If a death does affect a mandatory buy-out, insurance on the lives of the principals in the amount of their interest may be advisable. In *all* mandated buy-out situations insurance proceeds are at the very least a real convenience. In some mandated buy-out situations the insurance proceeds are absolutely critical. If a death causes:

- A buy-out obligation on the survivors.

- A predictably significant dent in future profits.
- Survivors who are cash poor and at their limit credit-wise.

This combination can be disastrous for all concerned.

Due to their inherent fairness (at the time of their creation, no one knows who might be the buyer and who the seller) the IRS virtually always accepts such buy-sell evaluations. Of course, the surviving owners and decedent's heirs are contractually obligated to acceptance. Therefore, there will be no legal or administrative expenses involved in evaluating these assets.

Life Insurance

Life insurance as a "product" for far too long a time was the scapegoat for the exaggerated public image of the life insurance agent as a high pressure pitchman. To whatever extent this image was justified in the past, it simply is not justified today. The consumer is too sophisticated for such methods to be successful.

As the result of a maturing marketplace the product (life insurance) is being given far greater respect for what it is (and always has been)—a valuable tool in both estate creation and estate conservation planning.

We just saw how life insurance functions in conjunction with business buy-sell agreements. There is not an estate planning guide in print that does not attest to the wisdom of insurance funded buy-sell agreements.

You also saw how life insurance proceeds can eliminate the legal and administrative costs incurred in estate sale asset liquidations. Incidentally, the loss incurred in estate sales is not limited to the legal and administrative expenses incurred.

Even if you get a fair price for your nonliquid assets within a minimum of legal or administrative costs, you will still lose the future appreciation of the asset.

Anyone who sold a piece of real estate several years ago to pay estate taxes can tell you how much paying the taxes has really cost them.

In attaining everyone's first estate planning goal—the elimination of legal and administrative expenses—life insurance can be an invaluable tool.

Life insurance advocates are quick to point out that in endeavoring to attain maximum growth and income tax advantages, an estate is invariably "cash poor." This course can be safely and profitably pursued indefinitely *only* if there are adequate life insurance proceeds available to satisfy all cash demands—medical-legal-tax—brought about by one's death.

For the maximum benefit of life insurance proceeds, care should be taken to see that the proceeds are *not* included in the estate of the insured decedent. There is no point in adding to the estate you are trying to conserve.

Death benefits will be added to your estate if you possess any "incidents of ownership" in the policy. This holds true regardless of who the named beneficiary might be.

An incident of ownership might be defined as having the ability to take action which would legally affect, either directly or indirectly, any of the policy's provisions. Principal among these provisions are ownership and beneficiary designations along with cash value and dividend usage.

Taxation realities demand that the life insured possess no incidents of ownership in the policy. For the insured to do otherwise is to, in fact, name the IRS as a primary beneficiary of the policy. Depending on your tax bracket that could amount to a significant percentage of the proceeds.

THE BOTTOM LINE

In the final analysis, life insurance is nothing more or nothing less than an installment contract used to purchase money. If the death of the "life insured" will create a need for money, there is simply no cheaper way to buy it. If the need is temporary, a form of term insurance is best. If the need is permanent, a form of modern permanent insurance is best.

A high salaried executive or professional will frequently "insure" his projected pre-retirement income. If Dr. Good foresees earning $500,000 between now and his retirement he would purchase a $500,000 term policy on his life.

The rationale for such a purchase is simple. The "loss" of the premiums paid should he live to retirement is literally microscopic compared to the income lost if he doesn't.

It is the very same logic that is behind a company protecting itself through the purchase of key-man life insurance on its executives. Selective key-man life insurance is almost universally recommended by management consultants and CPAs.

The illustration on the following page shows how the key-man concept applies to both a business and a family in terms of insuring against a potential economic loss.

Probably the most significant contribution life insurance makes in estate planning is that of "financing" estate taxes. Generally, some form of permanent insurance is used. The life insurance contract for the purchase of money is one method of financing estate taxes. Alternative methods of purchasing money are an after death bank loan or, under certain circumstances, an IRS 4 percent "hardship" tax payment plan.

The entire last chapter is devoted to a subject almost always ignored by estate planning guides. The chapter is titled "How To Pay Your Taxes."

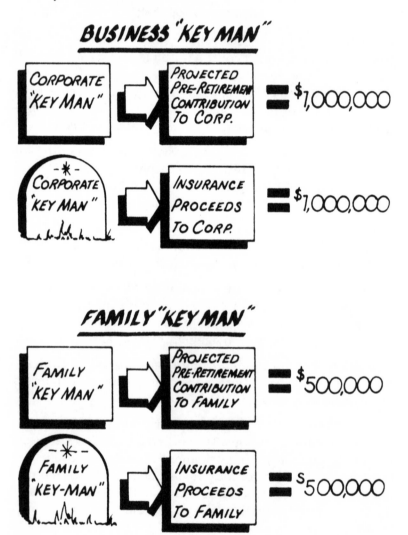

A Summary of Legal/Administrative Costs

You have now been given the tools (living trust, buy-sell agreement and life insurance) most commonly used to effectively eliminate nonessential legal and administrative expenses.

The attainment of this end—everybody's first specific estate planning goal—should be pretty much of an accomplished fact after implementation of these common estate planning tools.

Nevertheless, you should review schedules J & L in your "706" settlement cost analysis. If there are any legal and administrative expenses remaining, check with your accountant or attorney to see if anything can be done to eliminate them.

It is important to note that the steps taken to accomplish your first specific goal in no way restrict or compromise the range of options you have available for accomplishing any additional specific goals in the area of estate tax savings.

Elimination of nonessential legal and administrative expenses in most cases amounts to the elimination of virtually all legal and administrative expense. This *is* the first specific goal in every estate plan simply because *it can be accomplished without the estate's present owner losing any control, right of possession, or practical use of his assets before he dies.*

Such is not the case when planning for the elimination or reduction of death taxes. Aside from charitable bequests and the marital deduction, there is *no* planning tool that can reduce anybody's death taxes without a corresponding pre-death reduction of their estate.

QUESTIONS AND COMMENTS
LEGAL AND ADMINISTRATIVE COSTS

Understanding Estate and Inheritance Taxes

Estate and inheritance taxes are commonly referred to as death taxes. They are indeed the taxes alluded to in the old adage "Nothing is certain save death and taxes."

Essentially, estate taxes—Federal or State—are levied against the decedent's estate itself while "inheritance" taxes are levied against the specific heirs who receive that estate.

Federal estate taxes are simple balance sheet "net worth" taxes. Inheritance taxes are a form of "income" tax on the inheritance received.

In the sense that we income taxpayers understand them, there are no tax shelters or deductions involved in estate tax planning. A specific percentage of a decedent's adjusted net worth is subject to Federal estate taxes. Your actual net worth will be adjusted by the following factors: Closing or transfer expenses, the amount of marital deduction claimed, charitable bequests and the unified credit.

Transfer expenses are, of course, those legal and administrative costs involved in transferring the decedent's assets. The marital deduction (a genuine misnomer explained in some detail in a later chapter) is that amount of estate you can transfer tax free to a surviving spouse. Obviously, to qualify for the deduction the estate must be yours and not your spouse's.

The specific delineation between "your estate" and "your spouse's estate" varies from state to state. By oversimplification, in community property states each spouse owns one half of their combined total estate. In common law states, each spouse owns that amount of estate they personally earned. In the completion of your mock 706, your technical expert will determine your specific estates.

Charitable bequests are unlimited in terms of how much, but must be approved as to the recipient being a qualified organization.

The unified credit is automatically available to all estates. You might call it the estate's "personal exemption." Its purpose is to exempt smaller estates from taxation.

Death taxes differ from state to state. Some states have a federal type "estate" tax while others impose an "inheritance" tax on each of the individual heirs. Each state has its own tax rate schedule.

The states with inheritance taxes generally impose their lowest rates on a decedent's spouse with progressively higher rates for children, brothers and sisters, other relatives and friends.

While death taxes are "certain" for the financially successful (unless they leave everything to charity), through proper planning they can be significantly reduced.

Inheritance taxes generally start at a lower base than Federal estate taxes. On the other hand Federal taxes, once applicable, take a far greater percentage of the estate's dollars.

In the smaller estates (those not subject to Federal taxes) minimum inheritance taxes are incurred by taking what is in small estates normally the most logical course anyway—leave everything to the surviving spouse. Inheritance taxes generally are not a determinant in estate planning.

It is the larger estates—those subject to Federal estate taxes—that are the target of our chapters on saving taxes. The Federal estate tax is the tax we will endeavor to reduce.

THE 1981 ECONOMIC RECOVERY ACT

The greatest changes in the estate tax law since its inception were incorporated in the 1981 Economic Recovery Tax Act. A summary of those changes, taken from a select House/Senate committee report, is included in the appendix. A few of the major changes are worthy of mention here.

The first change was an increase in the Unified Credit effectively increasing the amount of estate not subject to taxation from $175,000 in 1981 to $600,000 in 1987.

The second major change was the introduction of an unlimited marital deduction. Effective January 1, 1982, spouse-to-spouse transfers in any amount were no longer subject to Federal estate or transfer taxes.

At first blush this change seems to be a real tax saver (and in certain estates indeed it is), but in many estates where concerns extend *beyond* the first spouse's death, we may be dealing more with sound than substance.

Let's first look at those who are certain benefactors of the unlimited marital deduction. In a nutshell, they are the couples who:

1) Have little or no concern about the taxes due on the surviving spouses' death.

2) Have little or no concern about who gets their original portion of the estate after the surviving spouse dies.

If, for any one of a number of personal reasons, you find it totally irrelevant what happens to the estate after the second spouse's death, implementation of this tax-exempt spouse-to-spouse transfer is designed for you. In fact, it is the end of your planning on "how to save estate and inheritance taxes."

On the other hand, there are significant caveats in the use of the unlimited marital deduction *if* your taxation and distribution concerns extend beyond the second spouse's death. From a tax standpoint, the total taxes on the estate may be significantly greater ultimately if taxes are avoided on the first death.

From an estate distribution standpoint, the first decedent forfeits any right or control over his portion of the original estate once it is transferred to the spouse. Their children could be virtually disinherited.

Let's look at each of these areas in a little depth, starting with ultimate estate distribution rights. No one but me has a legal right to distribute that which is mine. On the other hand, I have no legal right to distribute anything that is *not* mine. If my holdings have been transferred in toto to my spouse I have forfeited all rights to designate subsequent disposal of these holdings.

Sound estate planning "gets around" this dilemma of both providing security for a spouse and guaranteeing the children's ultimate inheritance by using what is called a marital trust. The trust acts as an interim "heir" for what usually amounts to the decedent's half of the total estate . . . after payment of any taxes due.

The marital trust is dealt with in more detail later in the book. At this point let it suffice to say it both guarantees lifetime economic benefit to the surviving spouse *and* ultimate distribution to the heirs of the first decedent's choosing . . . without being retaxed at the second spouse's death.

PLANNERS BEWARE!!

Maximum implementation of the marital deduction will preclude any estate taxes on the first death. However, in taking full advantage of the deduction, you are affecting a major change in the tax status of the marital trust at the second death. All trust assets in excess of the first decedent's basic exemption become an immediate part of the surviving spouse's taxable estate.

The surviving spouse's estate may be subjected to even higher tax brackets, and will have *no* marital deduction to offset them. All future appreciation of the "excess" estate will now be subject to taxation. In a nutshell, the additional taxes due at the second death could be far greater than the taxes saved on the first.

In the past, maximum estate tax savings have been achieved by both "equalizing and minimizing" the spouses' estates as much as possible before death. The primary tools have been the marital deduction as an equalizer and the marital trust as a minimizer (of the surviving spouse's estate).

This will continue to be the best course to follow in many, if not most, estates in the future, *even* if it means paying some estate taxes on the first spouse's death.

The third major change in the estate tax/gift tax law was an increase from $3,000 to $10,000 in the annual tax exempt gift allowance. "Gifts" are addressed at some length in a later chapter.

The fourth change involved a revision in the graduated tax rates. Beyond $2,500,000, the tax rate shall remain at 50 percent vs. the old rate escalation to a maximum of 70 percent of the estate in excess of $5,000,000.

YOUR DISCRETIONARY GOALS

As indicated earlier in defining estate planning objectives, there are two specific potential tax saving goals.

One addresses the reduction of "first generation" estate taxes. First generation taxation once again refers to the first time your assets are taxed—at your death.

The other goal addresses the reduction of second generation taxes. Second generation taxation once again refers to the re-taxation of those same assets at the deaths of their recipients, your heirs.

> The steps taken to reduce first generation taxes do so by either removing assets from, or precluding additions to, an estate. The less you (*and your spouse*) are worth at your deaths, the lower the "first generation" taxes.

> The steps taken to reduce second generation taxes do so by transferring that estate, entirely or in part, past either the surviving spouse (to the children) or both the surviving spouse and children to the grandchildren. The fewer subsequent estates your assets pass through, the less immediate and frequent their retaxation and the lower the "second generation" taxes.

Once again, when considering either reducing your estate or revising your post-death distribution plans, tax factors should always take a back seat to personal needs. However, all estate planning decisions must be made with an awareness of the tax ramifications. With these factors in mind let's look at our two potential tax savings goals.

QUESTIONS AND COMMENTS
ESTATE AND INHERITANCE TAXES

Reducing First Generation Taxes

The only way to reduce Federal estate taxes is to reduce the holdings subject to taxes. The way to reduce first generation taxes on your estate is to reduce your estate before you die. This is basic and clearly spells out what you must "give" in order to attain a reduction in first generation taxes.

There are, quite simply, only two ways to reduce your estate before you die. The first is to spend it faster than you make it. The second is to transfer some of it now to whomever it will ultimately be going to after you die.

As interesting as the first alternative sounds, in a practical sense it is usually impossible to spend it faster than you make it. If you will reflect on the growth of your personal net worth over the past several years you will appreciate this fact.

Since you can't spend it faster than you make it and you can't take it with you, an objective estate planner will urge you to reduce your estate through pre-death asset transfers.

While the mechanics of pre-death asset transfers are technically simple, psychological acceptance of pre-death estate reduction is not. You did not create your estate by giving things away. Conversely, you cannot maximize its retention by holding on to everything until you die.

The raison d'etre for considering pre-death estate reduction is, of course, the graduated Federal Estate Tax. To deliberately maintain or continue to add to an already potentially taxable estate—yours or your spouse's—is, in fact, to name the IRS as a primary beneficiary or principal heir of that excess estate.

Once again refer to the Form 706 estate tax chart for your present tax bracket as well as to see what percent the IRS will ultimately take of any further accumulations in your taxable estate. When you factor in State death taxes you can readily see the economic futility of further accumulations in your taxable estate.

ESTATE REDUCTION = TAX REDUCTION

The reason for reducing an estate is quite simply to save taxes. The reason many who should reduce their estates but don't is equally basic: They honestly don't think they can afford to do so.

Defining an "adequate" estate is a very personal and admittedly difficult task. However, in light of the tax ramifications, I'm sure you agree that if you wish to maximize your estate's retention, making such a determination is essential to the effort.

An "adequate" estate, once defined, is your specific goal for estate reduction and first generation tax savings. Your present position for planning purposes is quite simply your present net (taxable) worth as identified in your mock 706 Estate Tax Form.

From an estate tax standpoint, dollars held in excess of those exempt from taxation are excess estate. The more of this excess estate that can go to your children/grandchildren before you and your spouse die, the less first generation taxes your estate will pay.

At this point in your planning do *not think of your estate in terms of specific assets. Your present net worth and to-be-defined "adequate" estate should both be considered in simple "dollar" terms.*

No estate planner can tell you or anyone else how much is enough. It can be of some help to you, however, to understand some of the more common misconceptions that lead people to overestimate how much estate they need to maintain their independence and security.

EXCUSES, EXCUSES, EXCUSES

One of the most common errors is to evaluate one's security on the basis of present cash flow rather than on the basis of the potential cash flow the estate could provide.

"I can't reduce my estate, I barely have enough to live on now," is a comment heard time and time again.

After spending the better part of their lives working for the creation of their estates, these people fail to make the transition to letting their estates work for them.

During the creation of an estate it is common to minimize what one spends and maximize what one invests. The purpose, of course, is to create an estate sufficient to provide economic sustenance and security in your later years.

From the beginnings of its creation your estate is made up of a variety of assets. While you are working and building your estate, the bulk of your assets are growth oriented and not cash flow oriented. Your labors are producing enough cash flow so your investments need not.

Upon retirement this strategy is modified (or should be) so that your estate's assets generate the cash flow necessary to supplement any retirement benefits you may have. If you do not revise your holdings to replace your pre-retirement earnings, you can indeed feel poor because you are, in fact, "living poor."

To properly evaluate your security, look not at your actual cash flow but at your potential cash flow. How much income would you have, for example, if your entire estate was invested in high yield stocks, bonds and T-bills?

Another common mistake in evaluating one's security is to presume your security and life style are limited by what your estate can earn. People often will suggest they are going to spend it all before they die.

While such statements are usually in jest, there is nothing wrong with spending *some* of it before you die. Reducing your estate can be accomplished any number of ways, one of which is spending it on yourself.

One way of doing that is to buy yourself a guaranteed lifetime income through the purchase of a single premium immediate life annuity. In exchange for a one-time block of dollars, an insurance company will give you a guaranteed income for life. The income is made up of taxable interest and a pro-rated tax-free return of principal.

The older you are at time of purchase, the greater the annual income. If you were to project exchanging your entire estate for such an annuity (*not* a recommendation), you have an accurate picture of your maximum potential cash flow or spending power.

The viability of tax-saving estate reduction has been brought home to several of my personal clients through the following visual demonstration. At an appropriate moment in the interview, I will place a pile of 100 pennies on the desk.

After suggesting the client watch carefully, I casually remove 5 pennies and put them in my pocket. When asked if I have made a noticeable dent in the pile, the client's answer is always, "Of course not." With 95 percent of the pile remaining, the "difference" is literally unnoticeable.

The reality is that a 5 percent reduction in your estate this year, *whatever* its present size, would make just about as big a dent in your financial security as the removal of the five cents makes in the pile of pennies.

INFLATION FEARS

Among the most common reasons given for not reducing one's estate is inflation.

"My $750,000 may be a lot of money today, but what with inflation it may not be enough for me tomorrow."

Indeed, if the $750,000 didn't grow, this would be a valid deterrent against tax saving estate reduction.

The reality of inflation though is that, while it is the anathema of the consumer dollar—food, clothing, medical costs, energy, etc.—it is an even greater blessing on the investment dollar! Inflation offers the investor 20 percent plus real estate appreciation, 20 percent deeds of trust, 16 percent treasury bills, etc., etc.

The more money (investments, salaries, etc.) one has available and working for him on a year to year basis in excess of his annual consumables costs, the more he benefits by inflation. If one consumed $50,000 last year, a 10 percent inflation says they will need another $5,000 to continue their life style. On the other hand, their $750,000 estate, wisely invested, will most certainly inflate 10 percent also. It follows that they, in fact, have $75,000 more net worth to provide the additional $5,000 needed.

THE *ABILITY* TO PAY HAS INFLATED
TEN TIMES AS MUCH AS THE *NEED* TO PAY

The problem of inflation, one of the most oft cited reasons for not reducing one's estate, is in fact a most compelling reason why one should reduce his estate.

The most common objection to reducing one's estate is, ironically, the most compelling reason FOR reducing the estate.

"They will get it soon enough when I die, there is no reason to give it away now." The fact is that nothing could be further from the truth.

Keep in mind that the process of estate reduction transfers dollars from the highest estate tax bracket, off the "top of your stack." If you could have transferred $100,000 through tax exempt gifts over a period of years before you died but didn't—your heirs would *not* get it after you die. Depending on your ultimate tax bracket at death the IRS will get as much as 50 percent of it.

INDEED, IF YOUR HEIRS DON'T GET THOSE
(EXCESS) DOLLARS NOW, THE *IRS*
WILL GET THEM LATER

Considerable hesitancy in affecting estate reduction often results from a lack of knowledge that there are a variety of ways estate reduction can be accomplished. You don't have to give your children cash or, for that matter, immediate possession of transferred assets. They need not even KNOW of the transfer.

YOUR FIRST DISCRETIONARY GOAL

At this point in our planning, however, it is a bit premature to get into the details of "how" estate reduction can be accomplished. For the purposes of this chapter, the only determination you must make to establish your first tax savings goal is *if* and *how much* you can reduce your estate.

The question of how it is accomplished cannot be determined until you have formulated your second tax savings goal, vis-a-vis estate distribution. Should you deem it both possible and advisable from a tax standpoint to reduce your estate, let me assure you now that your technician has the tools to accomplish the reduction and at the same time eliminate any practical "negatives" you may now envision in the process.

QUESTIONS AND COMMENTS
FIRST GENERATION TAXES

Reducing Second Generation Taxes

If first generation taxation is determined basically by what you have when you die, second generation taxation is determined solely by who gets it.

The way to reduce first generation taxation is to reduce your estate. The only way to reduce second generation taxation is to change your present distribution plan. The purpose of changing your distribution plan is *to avoid unnecessary additions* to other (ultimately taxable) estates.

Maximum second generation taxes occur if your assets pass to, and are taxed in, the successive estates of your spouse, children and grandchildren. Minimum retaxation occurs if you bypass your spouse and children and transfer directly to your grandchildren. Your ultimate estate distribution will probably fall somewhere in between.

Once again, the fewer subsequent estates your assets pass through, the less frequent and immediate their retaxation and, in the final analysis, the lower the second generation tax bite.

A 70-year-old man, for example, can leave $500,000 to his spouse only to have the assets almost certainly retaxed in the relatively near future at the death of that spouse. As an alternative, he can leave $100,000 to each of five children where it will probably be retaxed in some of their estates in the distant future.

The same 70-year-old man has a third alternative—leave $50,000 to each of ten grandchildren where some of it may possibly be retaxed again in some of their estates in the far distant future.

Indeed the only way to reduce second generation taxes (the retaxation of your assets) is to selectively bypass certain heirs, excluding them partially or entirely from an inheritance.

A TAXFREE BENEFIT

You can, however, bypass an heir and still give him or her essentially the same degree of security that an inheritance would have provided. This is accomplished by willing your assets to a (marital) trust rather than to either your spouse or children.

The trust serves as an interim heir between the decedent and the children. It can, for example, legally guarantee a lifetime of economic benefit or income to a surviving spouse *without* that spouse assuming legal title. The children are legally guaranteed the ultimate delivery of the assets, usually at the death of the surviving spouse—taxfree.

When planning for the specific distribution of your estate, and addressing each potential heir's needs in turn, you have three distinct options to consider:

1. A direct inheritance.
2. Income rights only.
3. No inheritance or income rights.

A direct inheritance will subject your assets to potential re-taxation in that heir's estate. Excess (over 50%) marital de-duction transfers, even if to a marital trust, are, along with their "appreciation," added to the spouse's estate. Income rights *only* can be provided to an heir, without adding to their estate.

If first generation tax savings means "having less when you die," second generation tax savings means particular heirs will have less of "yours" when they die.

YOUR SECOND DISCRETIONARY GOAL

Now that you have a general understanding of second gener-ation taxes, let's look at some guidelines to follow in contem-plating possible second generation tax savings goals.

To begin with, in the *initial* planning stages both tax savings goals should be established in simple "dollar" terms—as though your estate consisted entirely of cash.

While the complexities of your asset mix do affect the actual implementation of your goals, this should not influence their establishment. Don't get involved in *how* to accomplish your goals until you have defined them.

Once again, the first step in establishing a tax savings goal is to establish your present position. Where are you now?

Where you are now as to second generation taxes simply sug-gests what is your present distribution plan and what are its tax consequences. If you have no present distribution plan (will or living trust) State law dictates how your estate will be distributed.

In any event, have your technician advise you of the probable extent of retaxation on your assets based on your present dis-tribution plans. His answer is a clear statement of your pres-ent position.

Contemplating second generation tax savings by changing that position, altering your present distribution plan, poses the specific questions:

- **Is revising your will worth any taxes saved?**
- **What must your presently designated heirs "give up" in order for your assets to incur minimum retaxation?**

To answer these questions, let's "rewrite" your will, again projecting distribution in simple dollar terms as opposed to specific assets. Bypass your spouse and/or children to the maximum extent practical.

Do not give anyone anything they do not need if there is a "next in line" legatee available to give it to. Having so done, present your revised will to your technician for his advice on the probable tax savings. Presuming that your revised will does produce reduced second generation taxes, have your advisor point out specifically where these reductions are brought about.

To the extent you feel that changes made in your will are an acceptable trade off for the taxes saved, you have clearly defined your second generation tax savings goals.

YOUR PROFESSIONAL PLAN

You have now defined both your first and second generation tax savings goals and identified your present position relative to those goals. It is time to instruct your accountant or attorney, armed with both your desired goals and an inventory of your *specific* assets, to isolate himself and draw up a *tentative* plan.

The specific steps he will suggest are designed to bring your estate from where it is now to where you want it to be; i.e., to accomplish your estate reduction and distribution goals.

This primary effort should be written in simple, everyday English for the sole purpose of advising you to what extent your technician can, in fact, bring your goals to fruition. To whatever extent he projects success, he will, in implementing the plan, draw upon the planning tools described in the next chapter.

Let me pause here to remind you that estate planning need not be a complex and time consuming effort.

Up to and including establishment of the only three specific goals any estate plan can have, you have had to issue essentially one order (to your technicians), make but two specific decisions, and one request.

The order: "Identify and eliminate all nonessential legal and administrative expenses."

The two decisions: How much you can reduce your estate before you die and to what extent you can safely bypass certain heirs.

The request: A tentative "game plan" to attain your tax savings goals.

However, at this point the caution flags are to be waved—frantically, if you will. We are coming to the point where o-so-many estate plans either bog down or fall apart completely.

Once you have established what your tax goals are, refuse to discuss anything with your technician until he has furnished you with his tentative plan, written in simple layman's terms.

Technical pontification on the part of estate planners is the number one enemy of successful estate planning. I would not even hazard a guess as to how many estate planning conferences have concluded with the client feeling so "out of it" as to wonder how he ever made any money to begin with! The result is usually, unfortunately, an abandoned estate planning effort.

Do not permit yourself to be intimidated by your advisors. The technician who will not provide you with a clearly understandable outline, in layman's language, probably does not want you to know how essentially simple his job is.

QUESTIONS AND COMMENTS
SECOND GENERATION TAXES

The Estate Planner's Eight Basic Tools

Once again the basic simplicity of estate planning becomes evident. Plan after plan after plan is implemented using combinations of the same eight basic tools. In point of fact, probably some 80 percent of all estate plans are set up using but four—the trust, marital deduction, gift right and life insurance.

If you plan on being an estate planner yourself, an intimate technical knowledge of these tools is essential. If you merely want your own estate planned, it is essential only to have a practical understanding of how these tools can help accomplish your goals.

The business man who installs a computer system is not as concerned with how the system functions technically as he is with what it accomplishes. That it saves him time and money justifies its use even though its technicalities remain a mystery to him. He leaves the mechanics of installation and maintenance to the technician.

Estate planning is no different than business planning, in

terms of an in-depth technical understanding of these, the eight basic tools:

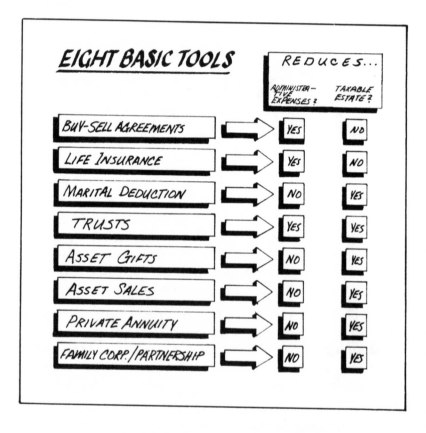

A "TECHNICIAN" OR A PLANNER

Your estate plan does not require you to have any more technical expertise than the businessman has computer expertise. You need only understand what a tool accomplishes while you leave the technicalities of installation and maintenance to your technician, the attorney or the accountant.

While experience suggests that it is a rare technician indeed who both understands and follows the basic concepts of planning, his expertise *is* essential to the proper installation and maintenance of an estate plan.

Though the entire effort may at times seem a bit complex to you—it is not so to an experienced accountant or attorney. Once **you** have established your goals—to whatever extent he can successfully attain them—your technician will do so by drawing from the same eight basic tools he uses in **every** estate plan he does.

To the technical professional, implementing the tools to attain your goals is *not* a complex and time consuming effort—unless he wants to make it so.

It would not serve the purpose of this book to present technical or legalistic elaborations of the eight basic planning tools. However, a simple explanation is very much in order. The following pages offer just that.

The tools used to eliminate legal and administrative expenses—the living trust, buy-sell agreement, and life insurance—have already been explained.

While the trust is, in fact, one tool, two particular uses of the trust are explained separately. Partnerships and corporations are for our purposes one tool—a family "business entity."

The Marital Deduction

Technically, the marital deduction is a specific "deduction" allowed on a decedent's 706 estate tax form.

As suggested earlier, the term "marital deduction" is a genuine misnomer. It is based on the premise that a wife has no legal right to any assets other than those she personally earned or inherited. Such a position relegates the housewife/mother to a position of legal serfdom. In practice, however, you will be hard pressed to find a case where a court permitted a housewife/mother of any years standing to be totally disinherited.

The marital "deduction" would be far more accurately described were it called the spousal allocation or share of the decedent's estate.

COMMUNITY PROPERTY

To better understand the marital deduction, you must first understand the basis of community property law (and how such law affects Federal estate taxes). Community property law, presently in effect in eight states including California, is the very reason for the creation of the marital deduction.

Essentially, what community property law says is that all property or estate created during a marriage belongs equally to each spouse regardless of who "made the money." If Dr. Jones brings home the checks while Mrs. Jones manages the household and cares for the children, community property law holds that each spouse legally owns one half of the estate created.

All 50 states basically subscribe to the obvious justice of this definition of ownership if a marital parting occurs by reason of divorce. There is no state where Dr. Jones is able to divorce his wife and walk out with all "his" assets, leaving Mrs. Jones destitute. Indeed, he would consider himself lucky to keep his half.

Yet, if a marital parting occurs as a result of her death, many noncommunity property states reverse this philosophy of ownership 180° and hold that the doctor owned everything and his wife owned nothing. The IRS accepts each individual state's designation of ownership for estate tax purposes. In actual practice, a widow's claim to all or a substantial part of the estate are likely to be upheld. But legal proceedings can be costly.

The Federal death tax ramifications were enormous in this totally inconsistent ownership "allocation" of the family assets as defined by noncommunity property states prior to 1948.

Let's presume the Jones family were lifelong Californians (a community property state). At Dr. Jones' death the family's net worth or "estate," all created during their marriage, was $1,000,000. California community property law holds that $500,000 belonged to each spouse at the husband's death.

The Federal Government, respecting the state law, would subject only the doctor's $500,000 to estate taxes.

On the other hand, if Dr. Jones' twin brother had the same set of circumstances in, say, Illinois or New York (noncommunity property states), his widow is faced with Federal taxes based on her mate's ownership of the entire $1,000,000.

THE MARITAL DEDUCTION AS AN EQUALIZER

To correct this unequal tax treatment of widows in noncommunity property states, in 1948 the Federal Government instituted the "Marital Deduction." Now the Illinois or New York doctor could elect to allocate half of "his" estate to the surviving widow taxfree through implementation of the "marital deduction". In the 1976 Tax Reform Act the "marital deduction" was redefined as up to the greater of $250,000 or half the decedent's estate. In January, 1982, the deduction became unlimited.

If you believe a widow should have no *inherent* rights to any estate in noncommunity property states, thank the Congress for its benevolence in enacting the marital deduction. On the other hand, if you believe she *has* inherent property rights, this "deduction" should be more accurately called the spousal allocation or share of the couple's total estate. *Her* portion is justly not taxed at *his* death.

Essentially, the marital deduction after January 1, 1982, allowed a surviving spouse to receive taxfree any amount of what local State law defines as the decedent's separate property or "estate."

Perhaps we have now come full circle with our "equal rights" as they pertain to estate taxation. Even before 1948, the husband in a noncommunity property state could claim complete title to a couple's estate taxfree if the wife died. Now, with the unlimited marital deduction, the wife can claim complete title to the couple's estate taxfree if the husband dies.

In either case, more often than not, the *estate's* best long term interests are served by using the marital deduction as an estate "equalizer" rather than a tax avoidance tool at the first death.

Significantly fewer dollars are subjected to estate taxation when the deduction is used to create two equal estates.

The following illustrations show how a $1,000,000 estate would fare using the marital deduction as the traditional "equalizer" vs. using it as a tax avoidance tool at the husband's death.

50% Marital Deduction
"The Equalizer"

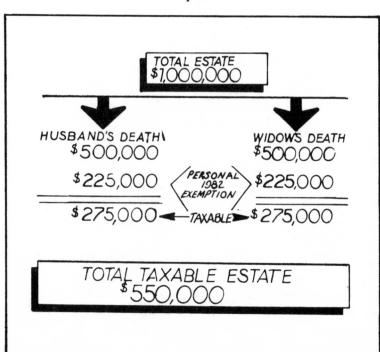

100% Marital Deduction
"The Deceiver"

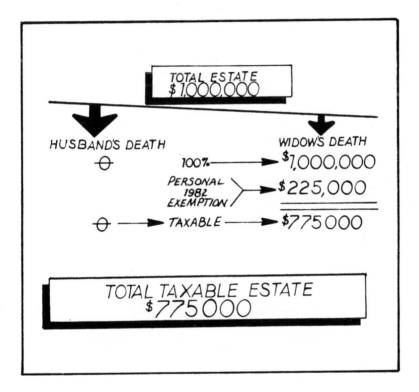

The equalizer results in two $275,000 taxable estates. The 100% deduction results in one $775,000 estate . . . $225,000 more taxed estate at a higher rate, thanks to the graduated tax rate schedule.

Trusts in General

All trusts are legal entities created to hold title to, manage and eventually distribute those specific assets placed "in trust." All trusts could be called asset holding companies.

Assets are placed in trust by a grantor (the one who owns them) for the single purpose of legally separating some or all of the specific property rights inherent in personal ownership; i.e., legal title, management control, economic benefit.

There are four essential parties to a trust:

- **The grantor:** (trustor-donor) The one who puts his assets in the trust and establishes all its terms.
- **The trustee:** Appointed by the grantor to manage the trust.
- **Interim beneficiaries:** Named by the grantor to receive the income during the life of the trust.

ALL RIGHTS, TAXES AND OTHER OBLIGATIONS VESTED IN SAME PERSON.

ALL RIGHTS, TAXES AND OTHER OBLIGATIONS VESTED IN (2) TWO OR MORE SELECTED PERSONS.

- **Ultimate beneficiaries:** Named by the grantor to receive the assets at the termination of the trust.

The grantor can assume all, some, or none of the other parties' roles depending on the specific purpose of the trust.

All trusts are either intervivos trusts, i.e., activated by a living grantor, or they are testamentary trusts, i.e., activated by the death of the grantor.

All trusts are designated at their creation as either revocable or irrevocable. Revocable trusts and all their terms are subject to revision or elimination at the whim of the grantor. Revocable trusts terminate at a point in time or upon a specific occurrence stipulated by the grantor.

Irrevocable trusts, once activated, generally cannot be altered in any way by the grantor, or anyone else for that matter. Irrevocable trusts also terminate at a point in time or upon a specific occurrence stipulated by the grantor.

UNDERSTANDING YOUR TRUSTS

Trusts are far and away the most useful tools in your technician's bag. Virtually every estate plan uses them. Unfortunately, most trusts are written (and explained) in such advanced legalese as to be almost incomprehensible to the layman.

Be sure any trust suggested be discussed in the context of achieving a specific goal. Be sure also you clearly understand who the trustee, interim, and ultimate beneficiaries are and *why*.

Be sure that any formal trust document be accompanied with an informal statement explaining the essential points in simple English.

The two most commonly used trusts are the probate avoiding living trust (already explained) and the marital trust (explained in the following pages).

The Marital Trust

The marital trust, like all other trusts, is an asset "holding company." It acts as a receptacle for a decedent's assets for the purpose of guaranteeing a surviving spouse economic benefit or income without adding to that spouse's estate. The trust is, in a real sense, an interim heir.

It is an interim heir in that it holds temporary title to the decedent's assets for the ultimate distribution to one group of heirs (usually the children, occasionally the grandchildren), while it provides lifetime economic benefits to another (the surviving spouse). In this role as interim heir the marital trust provides the family with the best of both worlds. Presuming it was funded with after-tax dollars at the first spouse's death, it will not be taxed at the second spouse's death. The surviving spouse has as interim beneficiary of the trust, the complete use of the assets—the right to all income from the assets *and* emergency rights to use the principal of the trust to any extent necessary to maintain his or her health and well being.

Spouse or trust heirdom illustrated:

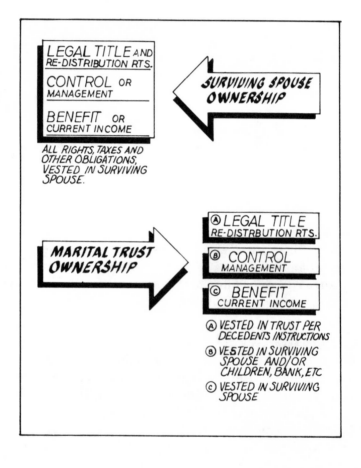

ANOTHER TAXFREE BENEFIT

On the other hand, the children or grandchildren as the ultimate beneficiaries of the trust receive the trust assets at the surviving spouse's death free of any and all taxes. They are free of taxation not because they were in the trust but because they never were part of the surviving spouse's estate, again presuming initial after-tax funding.

The trust legally guarantees the surviving spouse the lifetime economic benefit of the decedent's estate while also guaranteeing that the assets ultimately go to the children (even if the surviving spouse remarries).

In the past it was common to name a bank as trustee of a marital trust to "protect" the widow. Today, however, it is more common to appoint the surviving spouse and one of the children as co-trustees. Retaxation of the first spouse's assets can be dramatically lessened by use of this trust.

While in a real sense the surviving spouse forsakes legal title to the decedent's assets, in a practical sense he or she gives up little.

The surviving spouse has complete and total ownership of her *own* half of the original estate. (The presumption here is either community property or marital deduction implementation provided each spouse a half interest in their original estate.) The surviving spouse has all the benefits of the decedent's half of the estate *for life*.

The surviving spouse can manage the trust assets in virtually any way she may wish as long as she doesn't blatantly squander them. Such action is largely precluded with the children as co-trustees.

The marital trust and the marital deduction are the two most widely used tax savings tools.

Pre-Death Gifts

Some people believe they can simply "give it away" on their deaths and thereby avoid death taxes. If this were possible, there would effectively be no estate tax.

The IRS, of course, does permit you to give it away but for the most part you will pay a gift tax based on the same tax rate schedule as the estate tax. A limited tax exempt gift right does, however, exist.

Gifts, tax-exempt or not, can be made of any asset of determinable value. They can be made directly to an heir or indirectly through the use of an irrevocable trust.

Gifts made to a trust can be made with or without the knowledge of the trust's ultimate beneficiaries, your heirs. The only requirement to "complete" a gift is that the donor immediately and irrevocably part with the asset.

Outright gifts, again tax exempt or not, are the **only way** you can affect a certain and immediate reduction in your estate. If first generation tax savings is one of your goals, the use of gifts is absolutely essential.

THE 1981 ECONOMIC RECOVERY ACT

The Internal Revenue Service, since January 1982, allows a person to give up to $10,000 a year tax exempt to as many people as the donor may choose. Such gifts are free of any and all taxes or tax reporting on the part of either the donor or the donee.

A husband and wife together can, for example, give $20,000 a year to each of their children and grandchildren. Inheritance tax exempt gifts vary from state to state.

These tax free asset transfers can be made, if the donor so desires, each and every year as long as he or she lives. One cannot, however, double up in one year to compensate for not gifting in the prior years.

Perhaps we are once again dealing with a misnomer in calling these pre-death asset transfers "gifts." A gift refers to something we have an option of keeping for ourselves or giving to another. This option does not apply to your estate.

The day will come (your death) when *by law* your assets will be given to others. The only options you have are determining who gets it and when.

There is a very real and practical reason for making this distinction in terminology between a "gift" and a "pre-death asset transfer."

The suggestion that one give some of his estate away *now* almost always is met with the following response:

"Forget it, they will all get it soon enough when I die."

The fact is that nothing could be further from the truth. If you don't gift it now, they won't get it later. If you can afford to give $10,000 ($20,000 jointly) this year to some or all of your heirs and don't, you are in the truest sense "willing" a substantial portion of those "ungifted" dollars, depending on your tax bracket, to the IRS. Predeath tax free transfers come off the top of your stack—the highest rate tax bracket.

THE POWER OF POSITIVE TERMINOLOGY

The use of the "positive" terminology—a "tax free pre-death asset transfer"—would inspire far greater use of this unique planning tool.

If tax exempt gifts are mandatory in reducing first generation taxes, additional (taxable) gifts are also a superb planning tool, to that same end, due to their inherent simplicity of implementation.

A $100,000 taxable gift of real estate now will remove any appreciation between now and your death from your taxable estate. As a general rule, assets subject to high appreciation are number one candidates for gifting.

Do not gift assets that may *depreciate* between now and your death. Your estate will not get any tax adjustment for such losses to offset any gift taxes paid.

If you would like to reduce your taxable estate on the one hand, but do not wish to risk jeopardizing your children's self reliance and initiative on the other, consider gifting to an irrevocable trust.

Confidential gifts of any type of asset may be made to the trust now for eventual distribution to your children at some predetermined future time . . . their 40th birthday, their marriage, your death, etc.

Your banker, attorney, or CPA should serve as trustee to provide independent 3rd party control. At the onset, you set up the basic investment and management guidelines the trustee must follow. You also maintain the right to change trustees.

If tax saving pre-death asset transfers are practicable, it is not so important how they are made as it is THAT they are made. You may gift some of your present investments (check for possible capital gains liability) or you may gift cash.

Your stockbroker can suggest any number of $10,000 investment portfolios designed to meet any risk/return desired.

Your real estate broker always has an unlimited variety of properties and limited partnership opportunities available.

If you are of a more conservative nature, you may wish to have contractual guarantees for your gifted dollars. If so, ask your insurance broker to show you how his newest interest sensitive vanishing premium contract serves as an estate transfer vehicle. If you can qualify, an investment in his contract will generate a return of up to 500% or more free of any taxation.

If you are really serious about reducing estate taxes, some form of gifting is essential. Some of your estate must "go" before you do. It is as simple as that.

Asset Sales

The essence of an asset sale to an heir is simplicity itself. You transfer title to an asset in exchange for cash or a note. Be advised that such sales must be of an "arms length" nature. If you do not receive a fair price for the asset sold, the IRS will treat the difference as a gift, possibly taxable.

You can't sell a $100,000 building for $10,000 without the IRS levying a gift tax on the excess $90,000. The tax is paid by the donor or seller.

The gift tax, due in cash, is the reason an estate planner may opt for an asset sale to remove a large asset out of your estate. The best assets, as a general rule, to remove from your estate are those most likely to appreciate in value.

If you give a $100,000 building to your children, you will be liable for a gift tax. If you "sell" it to them, you can avoid the gift tax and effactually "give it to them" by using your tax exempt annual gift right to forgive their note payments.

If you need income, the sale of an appreciating asset to your children can both remove the appreciation from your estate and provide you with cash income through acceptance of their note payments.

The Private Annuity

One kind of commercial annuity involves the transfer of a large block of cash to an insurance company in exchange for a lifetime income based on the age of the purchaser and the guaranteed interest rate of the insurance company. Such a contract is commonly called a single premium immediate (payment) annuity.

The private annuity is essentially the same contract with two specific alterations. First, the annuitant substitutes one of his heirs for the insurance company. Secondly, he substitutes an asset (ideally one subject to high appreciation and/or income generation) for the large block of cash transferred.

With the commercial annuity I give the Ajax Insurance Company a $100,000 check in exchange for their commitment to pay me $400 a month for life.

With the private annuity I give my son a piece of property worth $100,000 in exchange for his commitment to pay me $400 a month for life.

The value ratios in a private annuity must be consistent with what a commercial carrier would offer. You can't, for example, transfer a $100,000 building to your son in exchange for an annuity commitment of $5 a month for life.

A PLACE FOR THE TAX PROFESSIONAL

The income tax ramifications are usually favorable but are rather complex and should be subjected to a thorough analysis by a skilled tax pro.

Estate taxwise, this is an extremely valuable and highly underused tool for reducing *taxfree* the first generation's estate.

In a commercial annuity if the annuitant dies prematurely, the insurance company is the winner. If the annuitant lives a long, long life the insurance company is a loser.

In a private annuity no matter how long the annuitant lives the dollar transactions are between different generations of the same estate anyway. There cannot be a loser.

The only loser—and an almost certain one at that—in the private annuity is the IRS.

If the reduction of first generation estate taxes is one of your goals, it is imperative that you consider the private annuity.

Incorporation and Partnerships

Both corporations and partnerships are distinct legal entities made up generally, of a group of people for the purpose of acting as "one person."

Neither of these planning tools can do anything to reduce your present estate tax liability. Both of them can do a lot in limiting the growth of your present tax liability.

Partnerships and corporations are commonly used in income tax planning and for purposes of limiting personal legal liability. Rarely, if ever, can the use of these tools for these purposes have any negative effect on estate conservation planning.

Properly set up, they should not deter you from minimizing legal and administrative estate transfer costs. Likewise, properly structured, they should not significantly affect your ability to achieve estate tax savings through implementation of other planning tools.

Both partnerships and corporations involving you and your ultimate heirs can be used to "gift" ownership interests at the comparatively low "now" value in order to keep the appreciation on the gifted portion out of your estate.

CREATE OUTSIDE YOUR TAXABLE ESTATE

In some estates, through the use of a corporation, it is even possible to "freeze" the value of your taxable estate. You and your spouse would hold all the preferred stock as well as the voting common stock. Your children (and grandchildren) would hold all the nonvoting common stock.

You and your spouse would exercise complete control of the corporation while any increase in the value of the company would accrue to the nonvoting common stock shareholders.

If you feel you already "have enough" or even more than enough, be sure to explore this possibility with your technical expert!

If a first generation tax savings is one of your goals, partnerships or corporations involving spouses and their children can be very useful tools.

If second generation tax savings is one of your goals, partnerships or corporations involving spouses and their grandchildren can be very useful tools.

QUESTIONS AND COMMENTS
THE EIGHT BASIC PLANNING TOOLS

How to Pay Taxes

As a general rule estate taxes are due and payable in cash within nine months of the date of death. The exception is when the estate's executor or trustee can convince the IRS that a timely cash payment would impose an undue hardship on the estate.

If neither cash nor reasonably attainable commercial financing is available to the estate, the IRS itself will finance the taxes through a deferred payment schedule.

If your estate's representatives have two tax payment options— cash or financing—to consider after you die, you and your estate planner have another financing option to consider before you die—life insurance.

To determine the best way to pay an estate's taxes, an objective analysis of all the potential options is in order. Specifically these options are as follows:

1. **Cash from the estate.**
2. **Post death financing—either a bank loan or IRS hardship financing.**
3. **Pre-death financing—a life insurance contract.**

The estate either will pay the taxes in cash and part with a large block of dollars all at once, or it will finance the taxes by buying that large block of dollars from someone else in exchange for a series of smaller annual installments.

These smaller annual installments will be made either to a bank or to the IRS itself as the case may be if post-death financing is used. Payments will go to a life insurance company if pre-death financing is used.

All financing options are not always available to every estate. The ability to obtain life insurance, our prepayment option, is contingent on the state of your health. Post payment bank financing depends on your estate's credit as well as the availability of commercial funds at the precise time the taxes are due.

Post death IRS "hardship" financing depends on the IRS laws in effect at your death. Objective estate planners recognize that the answer to the question, "How to pay estate taxes", is essentially simple.

THE ESTATE'S BEST INTERESTS

The primary consideration in determining the best of the available options is the comparative long term effect on the estate rather than the short term effect on the person making the tax payment. Nobody, now or later, wants to pay taxes.

THREE DISTINCT OPTIONS

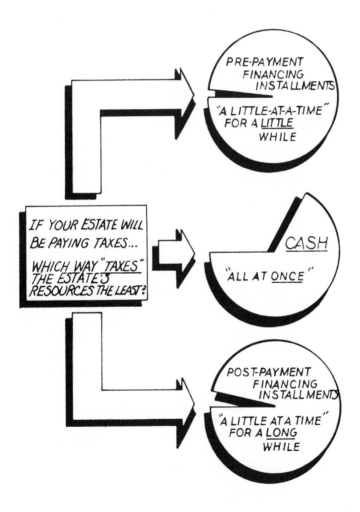

What's important to the estate is not so much who is around when the taxes are paid but rather how many dollars does it take from the estate to pay them. The fewer dollars used to pay the taxes, the more available for investment.

Let's now look at each option in turn.

Cash from the Estate

Cash is almost always the most expensive way to pay your taxes. As a matter of fact, cash is usually the most expensive way to acquire anything. As a result, creative financing is a vital part of all business or estate planning.

Financing is preferred over cash in all situations where the money you owe can earn more than the cost of owing it. Financing becomes cost *ineffective* only when the retained capital (the amount financed) cannot earn more than the cost of retaining it (the finance charges).

If I can borrow at 12 percent and earn 15 to 20 percent with the funds, it pays to borrow. Suppose I owe someone $100,000 and have the alternative of paying them off now in cash or spreading the payments over 10 years at 12 percent interest.

I may well opt for the installment plan if I have better use now for my $100,000. In a purist sense, the sole criteria for comparing the cash method of tax payment with potential financing options is: Can my retained or unpaid funds outearn the interest charges I pay to retain them?

WEALTHY AND "BROKE"?

Cash almost always is the most expensive way to pay taxes from a standpoint of practicality. Your estate should never be in a position to pay cash—and indeed most are not—without costly asset liquidations.

Most financially successful people attain that status because they keep all their money at work, locked up in various investments. The wealthy person will usually die wealthy in terms of estate but poor in terms of cash. To be in a heavy cash position is to sacrifice the earning potential of your money.

To die wealthy in terms of estate but poor in terms of cash is the way it usually is and, in fact, the way that it should be—*provided* that estate tax financing has been made an integral part of the estate plan.

It is indeed unfortunate that most estates do, in fact, have to pay taxes in cash from the estate after suffering costly estate sale liquidations. This is true simply because the question of how to pay the taxes was not a part of the estate plan.

Post-Death Financing

Once again, any kind of financing is preferable to payment in cash as long as the retained capital can out-earn the cost of retaining it. Naturally, the lower the interest rate the more attractive and profitable it is to finance the taxes.

Our two sources for post death financing are commercial loans and IRS "hardship" financing. It is not our purpose to get into the nitty-gritty of commercial financing. Let it suffice to say this option would depend solely on your estate's ability to secure a loan at acceptable terms at the time the taxes are due.

Let's look at the less familiar IRS financing. Rather than get involved in the details of qualifying for IRS "hardship" payment plans, let your legal technician advise you as to whether your estate can qualify or not. Let it suffice here to repeat that IRS deferred payment plans are available where a timely cash payment of the estate tax would impose an undue hardship on the estate.

NOW EASIER THAN EVER

Inasmuch as what the IRS originally meant by undue hardship has in actual practice evolved into significant inconvenience, more and more estates are qualifying for one or the other of two basic IRS plans.

If you should qualify, the first plan offers up to 10 year financing at a rate of interest (revised every couple of years) intended to approximate the prevailing prime rate.

The second plan, should your estate qualify, offers interest payments only (at 4 percent) for up to five years, and principal payments, at 4 percent, over the succeeding 10 years. It obviously is a bit more difficult to "qualify" for this plan.

Either plan, if available, will preclude the necessity of your estate's parting with a large block of dollars when filing the 706 Estate Tax Form.

The illustration on the following page shows the annual installments required to pay a $100,000 estate tax with each of the two IRS "hardship" payment plans.

Once again, these plans are available only under certain conditions. For example, the IRS will not force you to sell the farm or liquidate your business to pay estate taxes.

Certainly no one can complain about the IRS offering them less than prime rate financing. Anyone who would turn down 4 percent financing in this day and age probably also would buy the Brooklyn Bridge.

YEAR	10 YRS @ 12% (Prime)	YEAR	15 YRS @ 4%
1	$ 17,220	1	$ 4,000
2	"	2	"
3	"	3	"
4	"	4	"
5	"	5	"
6	"	6	14,000
7	"	7	13,600
8	"	8	13,200
9	"	9	12,800
10	"	10	12,400
	$172,200	11	12,000
		12	11,600
		13	11,200
		14	10,800
		15	10,400
			$142,000

Pre-Death Financing

The third option for paying estate taxes is to finance them with a pre-payment installment contract—life insurance. Rather than "buying" a block of cash from a bank or the IRS with a series of installment payments after your death, you "buy" the cash from an insurance company with a series of installment payments before your death.

While life insurance is not commonly thought of as a finance or installment contract, it indeed is exactly that: "The exchange between two parties of an obligation of a large block of dollars at one point in time for a series of smaller installments over an extended period of time."

There is *no essential difference* in the three financing alternatives as installment purchases of money. In all cases your estate is trading off to someone else the obligation of a large block of dollars at one point in time in exchange for your estate's commitment to a series of smaller annual installments.

Whatever you call it—a prepayment installment contract or a life insurance policy—the contract in essence is an installment purchase of money. Its purchase *now* will preclude the necessity of sacrificing any assets or borrowing money later.

The number of prepayment contracts, or life insurance policies, on the market today is staggering, to say the least. A good prepayment contract for $100,000 in taxes will approximate the costs suggested in the following chart.

The following figures were provided by a major life insurance company. They show, at various ages, the cost of a $100,000 estate tax prepayment financial contract.

AGE Year	45	50	55	60	65	70
1	$ 2,850	$ 3,550	$ 4,450	$ 5,700	$ 7,400	$ 9,700
2	"	"	"	"	"	"
3	"	"	"	"	"	"
4	"	"	"	"	"	"
5	"	"	"	"	"	"
6	"	"	"	"	"	"
7	"	"	"	"	"	"
8	"	"	"	"	"	"
9	"	"	"	"	"	"
10	"	"	"	"	"	"
11	"	"	"	"	"	"
12	"	"	"	"	"	"
13	"	"	"	"	"	"
14	0	0	0	0	"	"
15	0	0	0	0	0	0
Total	$37,050	$46,150	$57,850	$74,100	$103,600	$135,800

The death that triggers the estate tax obligation also immediately completes the purchase contract for the $100,000 to pay it.

The cost of the $100,000 is the sum of the annual installments paid prior to death—up to a maximum of (approximately) 13 to 14 installments.

Selecting the Right Option

Most planners agree that financing pays whenever we can earn more with our retained capital than it costs us to retain it. This principle is the very essence of creative financing.

As far as financing estate taxes goes, while the date of your death will establish legally when the taxes are due, it does not necessarily dictate the best time to pay them.

When evaluating available prepayment and postpayment options, the objective planner recognizes that the particular calendar years involved in an installment contract and their relationship to the actual time of your death are totally irrelevant to the long-term interests of your estate.

He doesn't care who "owns" the estate when the taxes are paid; he just cares about how much it costs the estate to pay them.

THE BOTTOM LINE

All that is relevant to the planner is the comparative cost of the specific finance options available to the estate. Which option, during the calendar years it is in effect, diverts the fewest dollars from investment to tax payment?

THE REAL COST OF ESTATE TAXES IS MEASURED SOLELY BY THE NUMBER OF DOLLARS TRANSFERRED FROM AN INVESTMENT MODE TO A TAX PAYMENT MODE.

Your estate will either lose the investment potential of the prepayment installments before you die or it will lose the investment potential of the post-payment installments (or, worse yet, a block of estate dollars) after you die.

One of the most difficult jobs an objective estate planner faces is bringing his client to a comparable state of objectivity. Nowhere is this problem more apparent than in selecting the best method for paying the estate taxes. What is in the best long term interest of the estate: Prepayment or post payment financing?

Here again, possibly one illustration is worth a thousand words. To best compare these tax financing options, consider the following hypothetical case.

Let's suppose our client is a 55-year-old small businessman in excellent health. There is a projected $100,000 estate tax due upon his death. He qualifies for both a life insurance prepayment plan and 4 percent IRS hardship financing.

Which of these two payment options is in the best long term interest of the estate?

OBJECTIVITY IN THE EYES OF THE TAX BEHOLDER

First of all, in the interest of objectivity, we will take this decision away from the businessman himself and give it to those who will have to pay the taxes—his wife and/or children.

Secondly, we will "remove" the insurance company from the picture and pretend that both the prepayment and postpayment contracts are offered by the IRS itself.

After all, it matters not to the estate whether an insurance company or the IRS gets the payments. What is important is how many checks are written and for how much.

Pursuing our hypothetical scenario, the heirs would now have two specific IRS installment plans from which to choose. The payment schedules are as follows:

YEAR	PREPAYMENT PLAN	POST-PAYMENT PLAN
1	$ 4,450	$ 4,000
2	"	"
3	"	"
4	"	"
5	"	"
6	"	$ 14,000
7	"	$ 13,600
8	"	$ 13,200
9	"	$ 12,800
10	"	$ 12,400
11	"	$ 12,000
12	"	$ 11,600
13	"	$ 11,200
14	0	$ 10,800
15	0	$ 10,400
	$57,850	$142,000

In addition to the overwhelming cost difference, the prepayment plan is implemented *now* while our businessman is still a financial contributor to the family. The post-payment plan can not be implemented until after his death, a time least opportune for the estate to incur a new expense.

There is, to be sure, little doubt as to which plan the heirs would select and likewise little doubt as to the plan an objective estate planner would recommend.

While you yourself will not see the estate tax bill your death generates, you can have a lot to say about how much it will cost your estate to pay it.

Incidentally, with a little shopping, you can probably procure better "prepayment" (life insurance) rates than those illustrated.

Let the IRS Contribute to Its Own Tax Bill

A unique opportunity exists exclusively with the prepayment installment contract. It is literally possible to use dollars that would otherwise go to the IRS to pay the estate's taxes instead. Here is how it is done, step by step:

1. Have your children purchase sufficient life insurance on you and your spouse to cover estate and inheritance taxes.

2. The children must be the applicants, owners, beneficiaries and payers on the policies; neither you nor your spouse are to assume any incident or ownership in them.

3. Using your annual tax-exempt gift right, gift the children sufficient dollars to pay the premiums.

4. Advise the children that since you are gifting them the monies to pay the premiums, it would be nice of them to "lend" the policy's proceeds "when the time comes" to the surviving spouse. This will, of course, preclude

the survivors having to sell off any assets or borrow elsewhere to pay the taxes.

5. Further advise the children that it would be *even nicer* of them—since you gifted them the premium dollars in the first place—if they returned the favor and used *their* gift right to exclude, year by year, the notes due in repayment of the insurance proceeds loan they made the surviving spouse!

Eureka! By using both generations' gift tax rights you actually have financed your estate taxes with dollars that otherwise would have been subject to taxation at your death!

Were those prepayment installment dollars still in your estate at your death, the IRS would have laid claim to a significant percent of them depending on your ultimate estate tax bracket. The IRS has literally subsidized its own tax bill.

THE TECHNICIAN AND THE PLANNER

This example of estate planning, vis-a-vis "How to pay your taxes" is probably the best example in the book of the basic premise that it is essential that you know what to do and why to do it but not necessarily how to do it.

There is little question but that this is the best way to finance your estate taxes. You are, however, asking for trouble if you attempt to implement this plan without expert legal and insurance counsel.

Our "layman's explanation" of how the plan works presumes expert legal assistance has taken care of the myriad of technicalities that can negate all the tax advantages suggested.

While one should never turn over the creation or establishment of a specific estate plan to an attorney, neither should one attempt to implement an estate plan without one.

In the interest of a clear example and simplification we have talked of financing "estate taxes." In reality we are suggesting "prepayment" financing for *all* settlement costs—legal/administrative, funeral and medical, Federal and State income and death taxes.

QUESTIONS AND COMMENTS
PAYING TAXES &
OTHER FINAL EXPENSES

A Summation

A professional estate plan ends exactly the same way it began
. . . with the completion of a 706 Estate Tax Form. Compare
this analysis with your original effort. How much have legal
and administrative costs been reduced? If estate reduction is
one of your goals, how much in first generation taxes will be
saved? If you have revised your post-death distribution instructions (your will or "will" section of your living trust),
how much in second generation taxes have you saved?

The reduction in legal and administrative costs and first and
second generation taxes, can and should be measured against
the cost of implementing your plan. This measurement, the
difference between the savings and the cost to achieve them,
is a legitimate return on investment.

Your personal role in your own estate plan is not a technical one. You set the goals—your technicians implement the steps necessary to attain them . . . UNDER YOUR CONTROL.

Once again, do not be dissuaded by "offended" accountants or attorneys when requesting signed settlement cost analyses. You are paying "professional" fees for vitally important estate planning information. It is not at all unreasonable to expect this information be formally attested to. The truly unfortunate aspect is that you should have to ask in the first place.

Objective estate planning definitely requires a psychological adjustment on the part of the estate's present owner. Estate conservation can only be accomplished if the present owner can separate himself in a psychological sense from his estate. He must be able and willing to look at the estate from the outside.

Initially, during the creation of your estate, working to satisfy your needs for both a good life and economic security, your estate's best interests were synonymous with your own personal interests.

Having achieved these goals, you now are in a whole new ballgame. Your estate's best interests are no longer in accord with your *previously defined* personal best interests. Quite simply, your estate's best interests may dictate that you give things away now and pay some tax bills that you are not obligated to pay.

After spending the better part of your life working for (the creation of) your estate, your success now dictates a sort of role reversal. It is now time to let your estate work for you, first and foremost—and then for its own conservation.

In a nutshell, successful estate conservation can only occur if you will allow your planners to implement those steps that will "attain the maximum estate retention for one's heirs consistent with maintaining one's own total financial independence and security."

The United States Estate Tax

The U.S. Estate Tax is essentially a net worth tax levied on the estate of certain decedents. Federal law requires that a U.S. Estate Tax Form 706 be filed on behalf of any decedent U.S. citizen or resident with a gross estate in excess of the following amounts: $325,000 in 1984; $400,000 in 1985; $500,000 in 1986; $600,000 after January 1, 1987.

Responsibility for filing the Form 706 lies with the estate's executor, or the person(s) in actual or constructive possession of the assets, such as the successor trustee of a living trust. Generally, the form must be filed within nine months of the decedent's death.

The Estate Tax Form 706, like most other tax forms, can be a bit intimidating. For this reason the following explanation is offered to make the form a little easier to understand. It is not, however, intended to supplant professional legal or tax counsel. Since you will be using the Form 706 in your planning efforts for purposes of identifying potential settlement costs, though you need not know how to fill in all the blanks, you should understand what the figures represent.

The easiest way to explain this particular tax form is to break it down into its essential parts:

1) Accumulating the Assets
2) Accumulating the Liabilities
3) Calculating the Gross Estate Tax
4) Listing all Applicable Tax Credits
5) Establishing the Net Estate Tax

Before addressing the form, one area deserves special attention. No part of estate planning is more misunderstood and causes more confusion than *gifts* (also referred to as *transfers before death*).

As far as the IRS is concerned, there are only two kinds of gifts, *taxable* and *non-taxable*. The determination has nothing to do with the kind of asset transferred, but is solely dependent on the dollar value of the transfer.

Non-taxable gifts are never of any concern to the IRS; not when they are made and not when the decedent's 706 form is being filed. Non-taxable gifts need never be reported on any tax form.

Taxable gifts, on the other hand, must always be reported to the IRS. They must be reported and taxes must be paid on an annual basis. They must be reported again on the decedent's estate tax form.

The overwhelming majority of estates are not involved in taxable gift giving, but many are (and many more should be) involved in non-taxable gift giving.

Present non-taxable gift limits are $10,000 per year per donee. There are no limits to the number or relationship of donees. A husband and wife may jointly double this amount. An unlimited exclusion is also allowed for certain medical expenses and school tuition. Prior to 1982 non-taxable gifts were limited to $3,000 ($6,000 jointly) per year per donee.

All gifts in excess of the prescribed limits in effect when the gifting took place are taxable gifts. These are the gifts to which the U.S. Estate Tax Form 706 refers.

Having set the stage, let's now examine Line 1 through Line 23 on Form 706, the United States Estate Tax Form.

ACCUMULATING THE ASSETS

Line 1

The entry on Line 1 represents the gross value of the estate before allowing for any liabilities or debts. Included in this figure is all property in which the decedent had an interest (including real property outside the U.S.) as well as, in general, the "when gifted" value of all taxable gifts made over the years. Credits are allowed later for gift taxes already paid.

There are nine separate schedules, A through I, included in the 706 form used to list and evaluate the decedent's gross estate:

A Real Estate
B Stocks and Bonds
C Mortgages Receivable, Notes and Cash
D Insurance on the Decedent's Life
E Jointly Owned Property
F Other Miscellaneous Property
G Transfers (Gifts) During Decedent's Life
H Powers of Appointment
I Annuities

No tangible asset can escape those schedules. The IRS definitely leaves no stone unturned in its effort to account for all the decedent's assets.

ACCUMULATING THE LIABILITIES

Line 2

The entry on Line 2 represents the total allowable deductions from the gross estate. These deductions are stricly limited to the decedent's debts, expenses and losses incurred during administration, and spousal and charitable bequests. Details are accumulated on the five following schedules:

J Funeral and Administrative Expenses on Probate Estate

K Debts, Mortgages, and Liens Owed by the Decedent

L Unreimbursed Losses and Expenses on Non-Probate Estate

M Spousal Bequests

O Charitable Bequests

You may note that the only deductions also seen on your more familiar income tax return are unreimbursed losses and charitable bequests. There are none of the other familiar writeoffs.

Particular attention is directed to schedules J and L. These are the heart of your usage of the 706 form for a dry run settlement cost analysis. Both your beginning and concluding 706 cost analyses should have those schedules completed and attested to via signature by your selected tax expert, your CPA or attorney.

CALCULATING THE GROSS ESTATE TAX

The Gross Estate Tax defined would be that amount of tax assessed against the estate prior to the application of all allowable tax credits. Lines 3 through 8 are used to arrive at the Gross Estate Tax.

Line 3

The entry on Line 3 represents the difference between Line

1, the Gross Estate, and Line 2, the Total Allowable Deductions. This figure is the taxable estate, unadjusted.

Line 4

This figure is an adjustment to Line 3 (when applicable), represented by certain taxable gifts made specifically after December 31, 1976. Now is a good time to point out that if the estate was *ever* involved in taxable gifts, the layman should defer completely to the tax expert in completing all gift-related entries in the 706 tax computation or any of its sub schedules. The word "complex" takes on a whole new dimension when used in reference to ever changing gift tax rules and regulations.

Line 5

The entry on this line is the total of Line 3, the Taxable Estate, and Line 4, a specific (and rare) gift related adjustment. This is the figure, the *Adjusted Taxable Estate*, upon which the tentative tax on Line 6 is based.

Line 6

This entry represents the tentative tax and is arrived at by applying Tax Table A in the 706 instructions to the figure on Line 5. The word "tentative" alludes to another possible gift-related entry on Line 7, and the application of various credits addressed on Lines 9 through 17.

Line 7

This entry is used to record certain gift taxes payable with respect to post-December 31, 1976 gifts . . . again a job for the tax professional.

Line 8

This entry, arrived at by subtracting Line 7 from Line 6, represents the Gross Estate Tax before listing applicable tax credits.

LISTING ALL APPLICABLE TAX CREDITS

Line 9

This entry, the Unified Credit, is taken directly from Table B in the 706 instructions. The figure is the same for all estates, and is determined by the calendar year death occurred.

Line 10

This entry is used to modify or reduce the allowable Unified Credit entered on Line 9 if the decedent claimed a special exemption for certain gifts (again) made between 9/8/76 and 1/1/77. That is no misprint, it does indeed reflect an 83-day period where maybe one estate (probably within thousands) made taxable gifts that will modify their allowable Unified Credit.

Line 11

This results entry is the Allowable Unified Credit arrived at by subtracting Line 10 from Line 9. The Unified Credit, every estate's "personal exemption," effectively offsets any estate taxes due on estates of $600,000 in and after 1987; $500,000 in 1986; $400,000 in 1985; and $325,000 in 1984.

Line 12

This entry reflects any tax still due after subtracting the Allowable Unified Credit, Line 11, from the Gross Estate Tax entered on Line 8.

Line 13

This entry records the credit allowed for any State death taxes paid. The figure is taken from Table C in the 706 instructions. The credit entry cannot exceed the taxes due as indicated on Line 12. There are no tax refunds due if your tax credits exceed the Gross Estate Tax on Line 8.

Line 14

This entry, arrived at by subtracting Line 13 from Line 12, reflects any taxes still due after taking the two major tax credits available to all estates, the Unified Credit and State Death Tax Credit.

Line 15

This entry accounts for certain pre-1977 gift taxes paid.

Line 16

This entry is for listing allowable credit for foreign taxes paid on assets located outside the U.S., and included in the Gross Estate on Line 1. The credit is calculated on Schedule P.

Line 17

If the Gross Estate on Line 1 includes inherited assets, the estate may qualify for a special tax credit. If the inherited assets were subjected to prior estate taxation within a period of time either 10 years before or 2 years after this decedent's death, a pro rata tax credit may be taken. Schedule Q is used to calculate the credit to be entered on Line 17.

Line 18

This entry, the last tax credit entry on the 706 form, is the sum of Lines 15, 16, and 17.

ESTABLISHING THE NET ESTATE TAX

Line 19

This entry is the bottom line, the Net Estate Tax, and is arrived at by subtracting Line 18 from Line 14.

There are two particular options an estate's settler may exercise that can effect the bottom line, Line 19, the Net Estate Tax. These options are addressed by Lines 8 and 9 of the General Information Section on Page 2 of the Estate Tax Form 706.

Line 8 asks the question "Do you elect the alternate valuation?" In determining the gross estate values, the estate's representative has the option of using either the value at date of death or the alternate value on the date 6 months after the date of death. The lower the gross estate, the lower the estate tax. The method selected must apply to all of the estate. The selection must be made before the 706 is filed. For this reason it is generally advisable not to file the 706 until after 6 months.

Line 9 asks the question "Do you elect the special use valuation?" In determining the gross estate values, certain farm and closely held business real property may be valued at its farm or business use value, rather than its fair market value. Once again, the lower the gross estate, the lower the estate tax. The appropriate calculations are made on schedule N.

Once again, this Form 706 explanation is not intended to supplant professional legal or tax counsel. It is a calculated attempt to uncomplicate the complicated. And, once again, you need not learn how to fill in all the blanks. But you must understand what the figures represent if you are to understand and control your estate planning effort. No attempt has been made to communicate all there is to know about the Estate Tax in all its minutia. A very real effort, however, has been made to extract the essentials necessary to intelligent decision-making.

APPENDIX

THE 1981 ESTATE AND GIFT
TAX REVISIONS

(HIGHLIGHTS OF THE SENATE
COMMITTEE REPORT)

I. Estate and Gift Tax Provisions

47. Unified credit

House bill.—The unified credit against estate and gift taxes is gradually increased from $47,000 to $192,800 over six years. The amount of the credit is $62,800 for gifts made, and decedents dying, in 1982, $79,300 in 1983, $96,300 in 1984, $121,800 in 1985, $155,800 in 1986, and $192,800 in 1987 and subsequent years. Thus, cumulative transfers exempt from gift and estate taxes increase from $175,625 under present law to $225,000 in 1982, $275,000 in 1983, $325,000 in 1984, $400,000 in 1985, $500,000 in 1986, and $600,000 in 1987 and subsequent years.

Senate amendment.—The Senate amendment also increases the unified credit to $192,800, but provides a five-year phase-in. For 1982 and 1983, the amount of the credit and the amount of cumulative transfers exempt from estate and gift taxes follows the House bill. However, the amount of the credit is $104,800 for gifts made and decedents dying in 1984 (exempting cumulative transfers of $350,000), $138,800 in 1985 (exempting cumulative transfers of $450,000), and reaches $192,800 exempting cumulative transfers of $600,000) for 1986 and subsequent years.

Conference agreement.—The conference agreement follows the House bill.

48. Rate reduction

House bill.—The maximum gift and estate tax rates are reduced over a 4 year period in five percent increments from 70 percent to 50 percent. The maximum rate is 65 percent for gifts made, and decedents dying, in 1982, 60 percent in 1983, 55 percent in 1984, and 50 percent in 1985 and subsequent years. When fully phased in, in 1985, the 50-percent tax rate will apply to taxable gifts and bequests in excess of $2.5 million.

Senate amendment.—No provision.

Conference agreement.—The conference agreement follows the House bill.

49. Marital deduction

House bill.—Present law permits a gift tax marital deduction for the first $100,000 of gifts to a spouse and for 50 percent of gifts to a spouse in excess of $200,000. An estate tax marital deduction is allowed for transfer to a surviving spouse up to the greater of $250,000 or one-half the adjusted gross estate. Transfers of terminable interests generally do not qualify for the gift or estate tax marital deduction.

The House bill removes the quantitative limits on both the gift and estate tax martial deductions and provides that certain terminable interests also qualify for those deductions.

Senate amendment.—The Senate amendment is the same as the House bill.

Conference agreement.—The conference agreement follows the House bill and Senate amendment.

50. Current use valuation

a. *Increase in maximum reduction in fair market value*

House bill.—Under present law, the fair market value of qualified real property cannot be reduced by more than $500,000 as a result of current use valuation. The House bill increases the maximum amount by which the fair market value of qualified real property may be reduced as a result of current use valuation to $750,000 for estates of decedents dying in 1981, $875,000 in 1982, and $1,000,000 in 1983 and thereafter.

Senate amendment.—Under the Senate amendment, the maximum amount by which the fair market value of qualified real property may be reduced as a result of current use valuation is increased to $600,000 for estates of decedents dying in 1982 and thereafter.

Conference agreement.—Under the conference agreement, the maximum amount by which the fair market value of qualified real property may be reduced as a result of current use valuation is increased to $600,000 for estates of decedents dying in 1981, $700,000 in 1982, and $750,000 in 1983 and thereafter.

b. *Predeath qualified use requirement*

House bill.—Under present law, to be specially valued, real property must be used or held for use as a farm or closely held business ("a qualified use") for five of the last eight years before the decedent's death and on the date of death.

The House bill provides that the qualified use requirement of present law, applicable to periods on and before the date of the decedent's death (sec. 2032A(b)(1)), may be satisfied if either the decedent or a member of the decedent's family uses real property otherwise eligible for current use valuation in the qualified use. This change is retroactive to estates of certain decedents dying after December 31, 1976.

The House bill also clarifies the types of operations that are to be considered "qualified uses." The bill divides these operations into three categories: (1) farming (including timber operations other than those that are incidental to other farming operations), (2) timber operations which are not incidental to other farming operations, and (3) other trades or businesses. The requirement of present law that each of these uses be an active trade or business use, as opposed to a passive, or investment, use is not changed.

Senate amendment.—The Senate amendment permits the qualified use requirement of present law, applicable to periods on or before the date of the decedent's death (sec. 2032A(b)(1)), to be satisfied if either the decedent or a member of the decedent's family uses real property otherwise eligible for current use valuation in the qualified use.

The Senate amendment contains no provision redefining what types of business uses constitute qualifies uses.

Conference agreement.—The conference agreement follows the Senate amendment.

c. Pre-death material participation requirement

House bill.—Under present law, the decedent or a member of his family must materially participate in the farm (or other business operation) for periods aggregating five years of the eight years before the decedent's death. On the other hand, if the decedent materially participates in the farm operation, any income derived from the farm is treated as earned income for social security purposes and, therefore, may reduce social security benefits.

Under the House bill, the material participation requirement has to be satisfied during periods aggregating five years or more of the eight-year period ending before the earlier of (1) the date of death, (2) the date on which the decedent became disabled (which condition lasted until the date of the decedent's death), or (3) the date on which the individual began receiving social security retirement benefits (which status continued until the date of the decedent's death).

An individual is considered to be disabled if the individual is mentally or physically unable to materially participate in the operation of the farm or other business.

The House bill provides an alternative to the material participation requirement for qualification of real property for current use valuation in the estates of surviving spouses who receive the property from a decedent spouse in whose estate it was eligible to be valued based on its current use. The bill provides that the spouse will be treated as having materially participated during periods when the spouse (but not a family member) engaged in active management of the farm or other business operation. Active management of the making of business decisions other than the daily operating decisions of a farm or other trade or business.

Senate amendment.—The Senate amendment is the same as the House bill.

Conference agreement.—The conference agreement follows the House bill and the Senate amendment.

j. Qualification of property purchased from a decedent's estate

House bill.—Under present law, only that property which is acquired from a decedent is eligible for current use valuation. The House bill expands the circumstances in which property is considered to be so acquired to include property that is purchased from a decedent's estate by a qualified heir as well as property that is received by bequest, devise, inheritance, or in satisfaction of a right to pecuniary bequest. This change reverse present law in cases where the decedent gives a qualified heir an option to purchase property otherwise qualified for current use valuation as well as in cases where the executor sells the property to an heir in the absence of such a direction in the will. If purchased property is specially valued, the qualified heir who purchases the property is limited to the current use value of the property as his income tax basis. This change is retroactive to estates of certain decedents dying after December 31, 1976.

Senate amendment.—No provision.

Conference agreement.—The conference agreement follows the House bill.

k. Property transferred to discretionary trusts

House bill.—Under present law, property owned indirectly through ownership of an interest in a partnership, a corporation, or a trust qualifies for current use valuation to the extent that it would qualify if it were owned directly. However, trust property qualifies for current use valuation only to the extent that an heir receives a "present interest" in the trust property. Treasury regulations define the term "present interest" by reference to the gift tax law (sec. 2503). This definition precludes current use valuation of any property passing from the decedent to a trust in which the interest of the life tenant (or any other beneficiary whose interest becomes a present interest before expiration of the recapture period) is subject to discretion on the part of the trustee. This result is the same even if all potential beneficiaries of the trust are qualified heirs. (Treas. Reg. § 20.203A-3(b)(1)).

The House bill provides that property meeting the other requirements for current use valuation can be specially valued if it passes to a discretionary trust in which no beneficiary has a present interest (under sec. 2503) because of the discretion in the trustee to determine the amount to be received by any individual beneficiary so long as all potential beneficiaries of the trust are qualified heirs. This provision applies retroactively to certain estates of decedents dying after December 31, 1976.

Senate amendment.—No provision.

Conference agreement.—The conference agreement follows the House bill.

l. Definition of family member

House bill.—Under present law, only real property that passes to qualified heirs is eligible for current use valualtion. The term "qualified heir" means a member of the decedent's family, including his spouse, lineal descendants, parents, grandparents, and aunts or uncles of the decedent and their descendants. The term does not include members of a spouse's family.

Additionally, the pre-death qualified use and material participation requirement may be satisfied by the decedent or a member of the decedent's family. Likewise, the post-death material participation requirement may be satisfied by participation of the qualified heir or a member of the heir's family. Property can only be disposed of during the recapture period without imposition of a recapture tax if the transfer is to a member of the qualified heir's family.

The House bill changes the definition of family member. The new definition includes an individual's spouse, parents, brothers and sisters, children, stepchildren, and spouses and lineal descendants of those individuals.

Senate amendment.—No provision.

Conference agreement.—The conference agreement follows the House bill.

m. Judicial review of fair market value of specially valued property

House bill.—Under present law, the fair market value or specially valued property, as well as the property's use value, must be determined for several purposes. The House bill provides for a declaratory judgment proceeding in the Tax Court review of Treasury Department determinations of the fair market value of specially valued property.

Senate amendment.—No provision.

Conference agreement.—The conference agreement follows the Senate amendment.

n. Credit for State recapture tax

House bill.—Many States have enacted current use valuation provisions similar to the Federal provision. Some of these States impose a recapture tax like the Federal recapture tax. Those State recapture taxes are not eligible for the State death tax credit of present law.

The House bill permits a qualified heir to claim part or all of any recapture tax imposed by a State which has a current use valuation provision like the Federal provision as a credit against the Federal recapture tax.

Senate amendment.—No provision.

Conference agreement.—The conference agreement follows the Senate amendment.

51. Transfers within 3 years of death

House bill.—Present law generally requires that gifts made by a decedent within 3 years of death be included in the decedent's gross estate at their value as of the date of death or alternate valuation date (sec. 2035(a)). In general, the House bill provides that this rule does not apply to decedents dying after December 31, 1981. However, the House bill continues to apply present law to gifts of certain types of property covered by sections 2036, 2037, 2038, 2041, and 2042. In addition, all gifts made within 3 years of death are included for purposes of qualifying for current use valuation (sec. 2032A), deferred payment of estate tax (sec. 6166), qualified redemptions to pay estate tax (sec. 303), and estate tax liens (subchapter C of chapter 64).

Senate amendment.—Gifts made within 3 years of death are included in a decedent's estate at their value as of the date of the gift.

Conference agreement.—The conference agreement follows the House bill.

52. Time for payment of estate tax attributable to closely held businesses

House bill.—The most liberal provisions of present law sections 6166 and 6166A, relating to the deferred payment of estate taxes attributable to interests in closely held businesses, are combined into one provision. The new provision permits deferred payment if interests in closely held businesses exceed 35 percent of the adjusted gross estate. Conforming changes are made to section 303, which permits redemption of stock in a closely held business to pay certain estate taxes, funeral expenses, and administration expenses.

The House bill also provides that the remaining unpaid tax balance will not be accelerated upon the death of the decedent's heir or a subsequent transferee provided the interest in closely held businesses passes to a family member of the heir or subsequent transferee.

In addition, the House bill provides a declaratory judgment procedure to determine eligibility for deferral and whether acceleration is proper.

Senate amendment.—The Senate amendment also combines sections 6166 and 6166A into one provision, but provides that qualifying interests in closely held businesses must exceed 35 percent of the gross estate or 50 percent of the taxable estate.

No acceleration of the unpaid tax balance occurs upon the death of decedent's heir or subsequent transferee, whether or not the interest in closely held businesses passes to a family member of the heir or subsequent transferee.

The Senate amendment contains no provision permitting judicial review of controversies involving deferred payment of estate taxes.

Conference agreement.—In general, the conference agreement follows the House bill, except that it deletes the provision of the House bill which provides a declaratory judgment procedure for controversies involving deferred payment of estate taxes.

53. Disclaimers

House bill.—The House bill provides that a timely transfer of property to the person who would have received it had an effective disclaimer been made under the applicable local law is considered an effective disclaimer for purposes of Federal estate and gift taxes where the other Federal requirements of qualified disclaimers are met.

Senate amendment.—The Senate amendment follows the House bill except for technical language differences.

Conference agreement.—The conference agreement follows the House bill.

54. Basis rule for property received within 3 years of death

House bill.—The House bill provides that the basis of appreciated property acquired by gift within 3 years of death is not adjusted to its fair market value at date of death if it is returned to the donor (or donor's spouse).

Senate amendment.—No provision.

Conference agreement.—In general, the conference agreement follows the House bill, except that it reduces the 3-year period to one year.

55. Certain charitable contributions

House bill.—Where a charitable transfer is an interest which is less than the donor's entire interest in property, present law provides that no charitable deduction is allowable unless the split-interest gift is made in certain specified forms. Because an original work of art and a related copyright are considered interests in the same property, no deduction is allowed for the transfer of an original work of art to charity if the copyright is retained or transferred ot a noncharity.

The House bill provides that where a donor or decedent makes a qualified contribution of a copyrightable work of art, the work of art and its copyright will be treated as separate properties for purposes of the estate and gift tax charitable deduction. Thus, a charitable deduction will be allowed for a transfer of a work of art to a qualified charitable organization, whether or not the copyright itself is simultaneously transferred to the charitable organization.

Senate amendment.—The Senate amendment contains no provison relating to split-interest transfers of copyrightable works of art. However, it provides a special credit against the estate taxes imposed on the estate of D. M. Kunhardt. The amount of the credit is equal to the smallest of (1) the total estate tax imposed, (2) the fair market value of the Matthew Brady glass plate negatives transferred to the Smithsonian, or (3) $700,000.

Conference agreement.—The conference agreement follows the portion of the House bill relating to the gift or bequest of a copyrightable work of art and the portion of the Senate amendment relating to the special credit to the estate of D. M. Kunhardt.

56. Certain bequests, etc., to minor children

House bill.—The House bill repeals the provision of present law which permits a limited deduction for certain property passing to certain orphaned minor children.

Senate amendment.—No provision.

Conference agreement.—The conference agreement follow the House bill.

57. Generation-skipping transfer tax

House bill.—No provision.

Senate amendment.—The Tax Reform Act of 1976 imposed a tax on generation-skipping transfers. A transitional rule exempts from the tax generation-skipping trusts created by wills or revocable trusts in existence on June 11, 1976, if (1) such wills and trusts were not amended after that date to create or increase the amount of the generation-skipping transfer, and (2) the testator or trust grantor dies before January 1, 1982.

Under the Senate amendment, the January 1, 1982, date contained in the present transitional rule is extended one additional year to January 1, 1983.

Conference agreement.—The conference agreement follows the Senate amendment.

58. Annual gift tax exclusion

House bill.—The House bill increases the amount of the annual gift tax exclusion from $3,000 to $10,000 per donee and provides an unlimited exclusion for amounts paid for the benefit of a donee for certain medical expenses and school tuition.

Senate amendment.—The Senate amendment follows the House bill in increasing the annual exclusion form $3,000 to $10,000 per donee, but does not provide an unlimited exclusion for tuition and medical expenses.

Conference agreement.—The conference agreement follows the House bill.

59. Annual payment of gift tax

House bill.—Present law requires that gift tax returns must be filed, and any gift tax paid, on a quarterly basis if the sum of (1) the taxable gifts made during the quarter, plus (2) all other taxable gifts made during the taxable year (for which a return has not yet been required to be filed) exceeds $25,000. If annual gifts are less than $25,000, a return must be filed for the fourth quarter.

The House bill provides that all gift tax returns are to be filed, and any gift tax paid, on an annual basis.

Senate amendment.—No provision.

Conference agreement.—The conference agreement follows the House bill.

Index

Buy-sell Agreements; explained, 43, 44, 45, 46
    ; life insurance funded, 45, 47, 48

Business Interests; protected by Buy-sell Agreement, 43, 45

Community Property; vs. common law property, 56
    ; creator of the marital deduction, 83
    ; determination, a job for your technical
      expert, 56

Estate Planning; defined, 1
    ; basic rules of planning, 5
    ; objectivity, 130
    ; eight basic tools, 78
    ; beware of "intimidators," 75, 76

Executor; the estate's probate representative, 39

ERTA, the 1981 Tax Cut; the major changes, 57, 58, 59, 60

Gifts; give it now?, 96
    ; pre/post ERTA, 59

Goal Setting; the only way to call a plan a plan, 6

Inheritance; effects on subsequent estate taxes, 73

Inheritance Tax; defined, 55
    ; vs. the "estate tax," 55

Incorporation; a way to freeze estate value without freezing growth, 104

Joint Tenancy; to eliminate probate, 31, 32

Lawyers; aptitude as planners, 7, 8, 74
    ; conflict of interest?, 8
    ; as technical experts, 20, 21, 32, 74, 102, 126

Legal Costs; a primary target, 10, 16, 51
    ; probate, 24
    ; second opinions, 21

Life Insurance; an installment contract, 49
    ; to fund Buy-sell Agreements, 45, 47
    ; to pay taxes, 49, 107, 108, 117, 118
    ; estate liquidity, 36, 37
    ; key-man, 49, 50

Living Trusts; a legal document, 41
    ; trustee–you or your banker, 41
    ; a probate-free "will," 40
    ; estate and gift tax ramifications, 42
    ; who "owns" the assets?, 42
    ; confidentiality maintained, 42
    ; day to day changes?, 41

Marital Deduction; a genuine misnomer, 81
    ; before and after ERTA, 57, 58
    ; origins, 83
    ; best use as a tax saver, 83, 84, 85

Marital Trust; tax-free ultimate transfer, 93
    ; the best of both worlds, 91
    ; a "holding company" or "interim heir," 91

Private Annuity; highly underused tax-saver, 101

Probate; the decision is yours!, 28
    ; purposes for, 27
    ; to save income taxes?, 26, 27
    ; an open-court legal procedure, 29
    ; avoidable via living trust, 26

Planner; the typical attorney, 7, 8
    ; the true professional, 7

Taxes, Estate; the 706 tax form, 19, 133
    ; how to reduce them, 60
    ; a simple "net worth" tax, 55
    ; how to pay them, 107, 108, 121, 122, 123, 124

Trusts; legal entities created to separate inherent property
    rights, 87
    ; the four essential parties to a trust, 87
    ; living, testamentary, revocable, and irrevocable, 89
    ; have them explained (in writing) in English, 89

Will, Traditional; an invitation to probate court, post-death
    asset transfer, 25, 26, 27

Will, Intervivous Trust; free post-death asset transfer, 25

QUESTIONS AND COMMENTS